T0064111

Pause, Think & Change

Pause, Think & Change

Amitavh Phukan

PARTRIDGE

A Penguin Random House Company

ISBN: Hardcover   978-1-4828-4734-5
               Softcover   978-1-4828-4733-8
               eBook   978-1-4828-4732-1

Print information available on the last page.

To order additional copies of this book, contact
Partridge India
000 800 10062 62
orders.india@partridgepublishing.com

www.partridgepublishing.com/india

CONTENTS

THE KIDS IN RAT RACE

I was sitting in my living room sipping a cup of tea with the morning newspaper in my hand enjoying the early March sunshine entering the room through the glass doors. My wife was busy preparing breakfast for our kid to go to school. She looked at me and asked me to go and wake up your son as he has to get ready and revise for the examination.

I had to drop the paper and go to the room where our son was sleeping. I saw he was sleeping peacefully oblivious to the schedule he would have as soon as he gets up. Though I did not feel like waking him I knew he had to get up and get going.

A obedient kid as he is woke up without much prodding, he brushed his teeth, finished his breakfast and got ready for school within thirty minutes. The poor fellow had to still revise for his science exam though he had studied everything the earlier evening. His mother was reminding him that he had scored one mark less last time because he had not done his revision properly.

My son is not the only one but almost all kids in the Indian middle class families is under constant pressure from the parents to score marks and come first since they start going to their school. Even if they score a 98, they are being asked why not 100, what is the highest marks in the class or how many students in your class scored more than what your scored in the exam.

If you stay in a big society/condominium where there are other kids who happen to study in the same school and class as your kid, and their mothers happen to know each other then there is a bigger problem for the kid. One of the main topics of discussion when the mothers meet is how your kid is doing in school and mainly what marks did your kid get in the test or the examination. If your kid gets lesser mark, then any other kid then, the kid should be prepared. Mother will come back and the kid will have to have a session or lecture on how the other kid is scoring better marks because he is studying more and not wasting his time playing with the friends thereby devoting more time to his studies.

So the parents put the kids under pressure from a very early age. The sad part is that stress is on getting the marks. I see very few parents asking their kids did you understand what has been taught in the class or written in the book. What is the difficulty they are facing if they are not doing well in the class, whereas the other kids are doing better. When a kid is mugging up what is written in the book and vomiting it out by writing the same in exam how much he is gaining or more importantly how much he is learning. Alternatively will it be not more useful for the kids if they are being told to understand what they are studying even in the process they score a few marks less as this will help them in the longer run.

I see and hear that during the time of the Board exams the kids are under so much pressure that they cannot sleep or even eat properly. There is a lot of pressure on them to score very good marks specially when they appear for their board exam in 10th and 12th so that they can get into a good college and get a subject (maybe not of their choice but what can take them ahead in life). With the passage of every year I see that kids are under more and more pressure to do well in these two exams. In our time we used to study the whole year round for these two exams but used to continue with other activities also like playing with friends in the evening, going to relatives place, attending social and family gatherings with parents. Today I see that when a kid reaches class X the parents become so serious about the whole thing that there is a curfew like situation in the house. I remember an incident a few years back when I had gone to Guwahati in Assam for a holiday and went to the house of my wife's relative. They had a daughter that time studying in class IX, so while talking my wife mentioned about the marriage of one of her cousin's daughter and asked the parents for how many days they would go as the marriage was to be in another city. The parents in fact were a bit offended and surprised and said you know next year our daughter has to appear for class X and so she has to study and at least one of the parents has to stay back though the other would try to make to the marriage for a day. So the parents have decided for the kid that she has to do nothing for the whole year other than study for her exams and one can imagine the kind of pressure this type of expectations and situation can put on the kids. In most of the cases if some kid is into say learning music or sports, class X can be the year when all other extra curricular activities or interests of the kids usually comes to a full stop as what they have to do from then is just study as they have to secure a better living for themselves. Now taking someone ahead in life has got a very different perspective for the parents in today's material world.

Usually it means you have to score good marks in your Board examinations, at the same time prepare for the various entrance exams to enable get into any of the professional courses like Engineering or Medicine, so that you can make a decent earning after completing your studies. The whole focus is on scoring good marks, and on getting into a professional institution so that they can make good money later in life.

I remember my own case very clearly though it was some 28 years back in the year 1984. I used to feel that I had a flair for writing and used to find subjects like English, Geography, Civics (Social Science today) quite interesting, though I was not bad in Mathematics, but used to hate Biology and Chemistry badly. In fact I used to just read my English books just once before the exam, in case of Civics just used to listen to what was being taught in the class, and still used to get very good marks in the exam.

After passing my 10th class I wanted to take up Humanities/Arts for my Higher Secondary studies and I mentioned the same to my parents. Though my mother was ok, my father was distraught and said what I was going to do in life by choosing this stream of studies, though he himself was a teacher and had done his masters in History. The only way to be successful and do something in life meant one had to study Science and then appear for Engineering tests and get into an Engineering college or get into a Medical college and become a doctor. I took up Science as per the desire of my father. At that time in Central School there was no option to select subjects so had to study Biology also for two years which was a nightmare for me along with Physics, Chemistry and Mathematics. In fact I never used to study this subject as did not find it interesting in any way and moreover our Biology teacher used to mostly read out what was written in the book, making the class still more dull. Appeared for my Board examination for 12th and when results came scored around 70 marks in Biology which included the 30 marks of practical, which was mostly a formality. That time admissions into the medical colleges in Assam was based on the percentage of marks secured in Physics, Chemistry and Biology. I had an PCB percentage of over 80 due to my high scores in Physics and Chemistry. Since my Engineering entrance results were still to come after the admission process for the medical colleges my father wanted me to fill in the forms and apply for the medical studies just as a back- up in case I do not get into an engineering college. That time I used to stay with my mother and father used to stay in another place as both were working and father was posted in a place called Dinjan. On the day of the interview and admission my father was waiting for me at the medical college. Somehow I was able to convince my mother that I had no interest in medicine and it was not possible for me to study something which did not interest me in any way. After waiting for an hour maybe my father called at our land phone and was very disappointed to know that I had decided not to take admission. He was not all convinced with my argument that I would rather do my graduation with honors in Physics rather than study something which I had no interest in. For him at that time only way to be successful and have a secure future was to get admission into an engineering or a medical college. It did not count that I did not have any interest in medical science and in fact it was a big hassle for me to study Biology for two years in 11th and 12th. When the results of the Engineering came my number was there is the list of the candidates who had cleared the exam and my father was quite relieved. That time there were reserved seats for students from Assam in colleges outside Assam, for branch of Engineering study which was not taught in Assam. I got into one of the colleges teaching Textile Engineering in Kanpur. The way the classes were conducted and we were taught I was never able to grow an interest for learning during my four year course in the Engineering college as mostly it was a monologue, and education was studying before the examinations and score enough marks to secure a first division. In the final year I started preparing for getting admission into a college for MBA. Somehow I felt if I do a course in Management than maybe I would be able to do something which is more close to what I would like to do in my life.

In all this running after career and making money neither the parents nor the schools teach things which will enable the kids to have a fruitful and healthy life and make better citizens. The parents and schools never teach the kids about the dignity of labor. This has a great effect in the later part of their lives. They grow up with the notion that there are many tasks which are not supposed to be done by them and they avoid doing these things throughout their lives. So a kid who has not been taught about dignity of labor will opt to have his house and its surrounding dirty unless there is someone who can do this thing for him as he has grown up seeing that these small things are not for him to do, or at other extreme what will people say if they see that you are cleaning the surroundings of your house. Also this lack of dignity of labor stops many young kids from taking up alternative careers once they complete their education as people may say you have studied so much, and now you are doing this. In fact it would be more practical and at the same time more fruitful for a person who is not good at academics to pursue a course and go to a polytechnic college or a vocational college where he could learn some skill that would enable him to be productively employed and earn a decent living much earlier rather than wasting five years of his life trying to somehow get a degree and then a masters in some subject which he does not enjoy and at the same time would not give him any good career opportunity. By joining a vocational college he would have learned a skill of his interest and would have started doing some productive work some three years before he would have finished studying something which at the end is not going to add much value to his career and life.

Another very important thing which neither parents nor the schools in India generally teach the kids is the importance of good health and the importance of physical activity in the life of a person. It is very important for the kids to know the importance of having good health to stay well. The parents should learn this themselves and educate their kids about the importance of having a healthy lifestyle enabling them to stay fit in later years of their life. The sedentary lifestyle where people spend long hours in office and then on the couches watching television and playing video games combined with eating fast food and aerated drinks and packed juices is turning the country into one which has one of the highest number of diabetes, a disease which is very much related to lifestyle and food habits. A little bit of physical activity is not only essential to keep the body healthy but it also enables the person to feel fresh allowing him to be more productive during the working hours.

I have been always a sports lover and like to play whenever I can. For the last six years I have been playing tennis four days a week after coming back from the office and I can say with all confidence I feel de-stressed and fresh after playing my tennis and having a good warm bath. I get a very good sleep and wake up in the morning much fresher than when I was not playing giving me energy to be productive during my working hours. Not everyone will have the luxury to play sports in our country, where there is lack of open spaces and playing facilities but everyone who knows the importance of some kind of physical activity can do simple things like walking, doing some work at home instead of sitting like a couch potato, taking the stairs instead of the lift whenever need to. Unless a person is healthy no amount of education and money will allow him to lead a good and happy life. A lot of diseases these days are related to the sedentary lifestyle and gaining of excess weight, as people do not take care of their bodies I know one lady who is a relative of one of my friend and amazed to see how a person can destroy own life just through lack of activity. There are 2/3 domestic helps available always in the house, so this lady does not need to do any house work. Whenever she needs something she has to call out to one of the persons to get the things even for a small activity like having a glass of water. The end result is she has gained a lot of weight and has to be on medicines. She likes to go on holidays but her holiday means going to a place and see it as much as possible by going in the car from one place to another. She will not go walking to see anything as her body does not allow her this luxury to carry herself for too long. What a pity just because of the lack of physical activity.

It is the duty of every parent and also schools to inculcate the importance of dignity of labor as well as physical activity as else India will be robbed of the demographic dividend. Economist and leaders say that India has a big advantage over the other nations where the population is ageing, as we have the biggest percentage of young and productive population but what is the use of this young population if they are not healthy and they are not productively engaged as they prefer to stay idle at home rather than doing some work which they feel is below standard due to lack of the dignity of labor. It is one thing to have the youngest population in the world but unless this young population is healthy and productively engaged we will never be able to utilize this opportunity and in fact this huge ever increasing population will instead of being a boon will become a huge burden in the years to come.

GROWING UP IN TODAY'S WORLD

Gone are the days when mothers used to have all the time for their kids and children used to be the focal point around which mothers life used to revolve. Today the increasing cost of essentials, requirement of gadgets, peer pressure has made it necessary that both the parents earn a living. With better education and opportunities definitely joining of fairer sex into mainstream is enabling the families to have a higher disposable income and afford a better standard of living. But at the same time finding a proper balance between work and home is very important for the proper growth of the children. It is not that it is the responsibility of only the mother to take care of children, both the parents need to contribute so that a child gets a childhood which is healthy and enable him to become a responsible citizen of the nations.

These days I see kids initially growing up with domestic helps and once they are a little bigger spend their time in schools, coaching classes, friends and their gadgets.

It is well known fact that the initial grooming of a kid happens at his home, but with parents giving less and less time to kids, this part of learning is missed by the kids and at same time their attachments with parents is very less. For today's child parents are required for fulfilling their demands of new clothing, mobile phones, computer games as this is what today's parents give them instead of love and time. In fact the fathers are much more guilty in this regard than the mothers. They work late hours in the office chasing their next promotion and higher increments. Even when they are back home they are too tired to interact with the children, or maybe something going on the television, they have some office assignments to complete or worse still he has to go out for drinks with his friends.

The first formative years of a child is spent at home, though these days kids start going to school at age of three, actual schooling does not start till he is six. This is a very important period for the development of kids as they are most of the time at home and children are very fast learners. Imagine what a kid will learn in these formative years who spends most of the time with domestic help. Not only this, it will be totally wrong to expect any domestic help to give due attention to things like whether the kid is getting proper nourishment, staying in a hygienic environment and getting the proper attention when required. As responsible parents it is everyone's duty to give as much time as possible to the child in this very crucial period of development. A child will develop a lot of his mannerisms, food habits, etc during this initial period. A child who gets proper attention from his parents and a healthy environment at home will have a very positive effect during this period.

Even when a kid starts growing and start his schooling, it is their home which has to play a very important role in what they grow up to be in their adult life. Let us consider a child who has grown up in a family where the parents have a good married life to a one where he sees quarrel between his parents on a daily basis. The child in the first family will have a much better environment in his formative years, will learn to respect the relationship between two people and later on will have much better chance to have a happier family life.

It will be seen in most cases that kids who grow up in broken families where they see their parents fighting most of the time, has a big effect on the kids behavior. These kids mostly have been seen to be not giving respect to elders, have lower self esteem and more frequently get into fights with other kids in the school. It has been seen that even with kids who grow with single parents, there are sometimes certain lacking like confidence, ability to be have a balanced approach, etc. If kids could have grown up with single parents nature would not have made family with both father and mother. Both mother and father is required to bring up a child and they have different roles to play in the upbringing of the kids, depending on whether it is a girl or a boy. A girl tries to follow her mother as she is her first role model and similarly a boy looks up to his father and develops his initial mannerisms from what he sees in his father or elder brother if there is one. I would like to give here an example of a family I know to illustrate the importance to quality time that the parents spend with young kids. This couple, has a very promising career, both having done their MBAs and working in good organizations. But their son was not doing good in his studies, though he was an intelligent kid his results were never good. The mother being a working one used to be tired coming back from office and father was always late going back to home either due to work in office or going out with friends. Before the examination mother used to sit with the kid and make him study wherein she would get irritated when kid would not be able to do his mathematics or understand what his mother was teaching. The mother also used to be in a hurry to cover his whole syllabus so that she could finish the household things and go to sleep to start her next day in office. This used to put a lot of pressure on the kid and the last minute study which was basically a self satisfaction of the mother that she had done her part by covering the entire syllabus without looking into whether the kid had understood what she was teaching did not help him much, in fact maybe it used to turn the kid into a bundle of nerves before the examination. Lately I have seen his father realize that he needs to give time to his son and try to understand why he is not doing well in his examination though he is quite intelligent. He has started to teach him trying to understand what is his lacking, giving him time and trying to see that his son understand how to do his problems rather than somehow mug things up before examination and the kid is showing improvement by doing much better in his examinations and in fact he has started to like his study and at the same time the bonding between the father and son is much better.

As parents it is very important that we spend time with the child and behave in a responsible manner. If a child sees that we behave badly with our domestic help, driver, neighbors he will learn to behave in the same way. A child tries to follow his parents and is greatly influenced by what he sees from his parents. Once the mannerisms are passed on from one generation to another over longer periods it becomes the culture of the nation. With a little observation anyone can see the difference when one is moving on the roads in Europe and in India. In Europe no one will try to jump a line while paying the toll or pass you from the wrong side, even in an empty road the driver will look both ways before moving on to the main road.

In our country, people will overtake from the wrong side given the first opportunity and jump traffic lights if they know there is no police at that time. In busy toll gates it is sometimes a nightmare as people will never maintain any discipline and try to get into the front by entering from either sides causing more delays and disrupting the whole process sometimes leading to ugly confrontation between the people. Places like Dhaka in Bangladesh is a nightmare for driving on the road where, everyone is honking and trying to find a way so that he can move ahead, in the process making the traffic even more bad. The bus drivers of the thousands of private buses will stop the bus bang in the middle of the road even if there is enough space on the side blocking all the traffic behind till the passengers get off and new passengers get into the bus. They stop their buses in the middle so that the bus which is behind cannot go past them, so that again they reach the next stop ahead to collect more passengers, with no concern to fact that it is blocking the entire traffic behind it. There are situation when people start driving on the wrong direction if there is huge traffic jams, thereby not allowing the traffic on the other side also to move also, disrupting the traffic on the other side and creating a chaotic situation whereby things come to a standstill.

THE EARLY YEARS

It goes without saying that the birth of a child has to be the most happy moment of a couple's life. It is the sign of the love and compassion between two individuals who come together after marriage and unite to give birth to a child. The mother has to go through a period of nine months of nurturing the baby inside her providing shelter and nourishment during this time. Unfortunately in many cases specially in our country a child comes under pressure even before he comes to this world. Still there is a huge bias for male offspring in villages and also in many urban families. It is a great shame that even today a large number of female child do not get to come to this earth. They are either aborted within the first few months of pregnancy or in some extreme cases killed after they are just born.

Science has enabled us to know the sex of the child before it is born, result many use to stop giving birth to the fairer sex. I for one do not understand why even ask the doctor if a child is going to be a boy or a girl. The whole fun and the surprise you get when you come to know whether it is a girl or boy that has come to this world is gone when you become so inquisitive. So the unnecessary pressure starts even before the kid comes to this world. Just think is this in any way required. The other day I was at a get- to- gather, where a would me mother said the doctor was a bit reluctant to divulge the sex of the baby. I asked her why did she want to know it. She said in that way they would know what name to think for the would be baby beforehand, I still failed to understand what is the hurry anyways as in Hindu family you need the time and date of birth also to decide on the name.

In today's material world people want to get a good job, settle down have the material luxuries and then marry, in extreme cases the young people are becoming so much career oriented that instead of getting into a relationship which may stop or hinder their career they do not want to marry and even and if they marry couples are reluctant to have babies. In country like Japan this is creating a big problem of an ageing society where less number of working people will need to provide for more non working people. Same is the situation in many of the affluent European countries.

Urban working couples think a lot and plan a lot before they give birth to a baby. Since maternity leave is usually for three months, so babies are left to be cared by domestic help in countries like India or put into cress in the western countries. We all know that till six months to one year the best food that a baby can have is mother's milk. Since the job does not allow the mother to be with the baby how can she provide for the first basic need of a baby. For a working mother it sometime becomes a necessity, but what about the mother who want to get rid of providing to the baby because she wants to go back to the lifestyle before she gave birth to the child, like going to her kitty parties, or join her friend in other activities as she used to do before the birth of the child. I think even for the working mother society has to think as a whole what could be the alternative ways so that mothers can at least take care of the babies for minimum time of first six months and maybe if possible for one year.

The most disturbing thing is the time parents in today's urban families give to the growing kids. As mentioned earlier the kids spend most of their formative years either with the domestic helps or in the cress. I even see when parents are going out station they will also have their domestic help accompanying them, so it is not only the time which prohibits today's parents from giving time to the kids, it has become the habit.

The kids are hence deprived of the love of the parents and at the same time not able to pick up the very vital early lessons which the parents can impart. I happen to know someone who works in a responsible position and the nature of work makes her travel within Europe and also to other parts of the globe. Once while having dinner I enquired her who takes care of the kids when she is travelling or working during the day in the office. She said that during the day the kids are in school which takes care of the kids till the father is free from his work and picks them up on his way back. While talking further she said that in fact she hardly gets to spend any time with the kids as she reaches home by 7 pm, then prepare a light dinner, eat her food and then start off again with the work which she was not able to finish at the office. During this time her husband would take care of the kids till they go off to their sleep. So she is depriving the kids of the time and love that the kids need from the mother and also not giving any time to her husband by bringing her office to home. I had to tell her that she was very lucky that her husband was doing all this for her, but she should not take it for granted as if this continues for long, not only she is depriving the kids of mother's love and attention but also putting a lot of pressure on her husband which could affect their relation. It could be fine to bring your office to home once in a while when it is totally unavoidable, but one should try to find the right balance between work and family, so that parents can give good quality time to each other and also the kids, so that the kids grow in a healthy family environment.

It is not sufficient to fulfill the material demand of the kids, in fact it is harmful to do so. Today husbands feel they are doing their part by giving expensive gifts and money to the wives, similarly parents feel they are doing their part by giving what the kids want before they can even demand it. By giving less time to the kids and more of the material things the attachment between the kids and parents are going down and at the same time kids today do not understand the value of money. They feel life is so easy, and becomes difficult for them to face the reality when it strikes them. It is very common for the parents to tell their kids if you score so much marks or come first in the class you will be given such and such gadget, so are the kids studying for themselves or for the parents. Once the kids gets into this mode of getting something when they achieve something, slowly they feel it is their right to get some gift that too an expensive one when they do well in studies or any other field. They do not feel that if they are doing well, it is for their own good and in fact it is going to help them only in the long run.

The kids who have grown in this kind of an environment where their demands are fulfilled at the drop of the hat or any achievement is linked to some incentive like getting a gadget or something take advantage of the situation. Their whole thinking changes from the beginning and they throw tantrums when they do not get something which they want, without any consideration to the fact that whether it is possible for their parents to fulfill their demands. These kids are in for a rude shock when they come to the real world where they have to manage with what they start earning after their education. In most cases they are not able to manage with the salary which they get when they start working and expect their parents to keep supporting them with money. The real world then seems very tough for these adults as they never heard no when they were with their parents. I have seen quite a few instances where youngsters who have been staying with mostly their parents till the completion of their studies, finding it very difficult when they have to go to another city to start their careers as not only they have to manage all the things by themselves including their food and other day-to-day needs but they have to also think about how to survive with the money that they earn. It comes as a shock when they find they are not left with anything after paying for their rent, their food and the daily commuting for work. In many a cases I have seen the youngsters unable to manage and come back home and trying to see if they can get a job in same city where their parents are staying as then they have the comfort of their lodging and food being taken care by the parents.

It is not sufficient to give time to kids, as parents we have to give whatever quality time we can to the kids. They should feel the warmth of the touch of the parents. It is said that a kid needs minimum of five touches in a day from his parents. The morning touch of the parents is very important for the kids. It is not that you have to pamper the kids, it could be smile, a soft peck on the face, putting the collar of his shirt right. The compound effect of these small touches is enormous. It makes the kids feel loved, they get more attached to the parents, they feel wanted and help them in having higher self esteem. More than the school it is the parents duty to teach the kids to show respect to the elders, behave properly with the domestic help or the driver, show tolerance to fellow human beings, learn to respect the faith and religious beliefs of the others, start respecting the value of time and money and other things which are so important to make a person a responsible citizen.

Someone had once sent me a very beautiful text which very well shows that what a balanced role any parent has to play in the formative years for the kids to have a good future which they can make for themselves. I am reproducing the same as I had received.

"A man who was a avid gardener saw a butterfly laying a few eggs in one of the pots in the garden. He started to look at it with lot of attention and curiosity. He saw the egg started to shake and move a little. He was very excited to see a new life coming up in front of his eyes. Every day he started spending hours looking at the egg. The egg began to grow and develop cracks. A tiny head and antennae started to come out ever so slowly. The man's excitement knew no bounds. He got a magnifying glass and sat to watch the life and body of a pupa coming out. He saw the struggle of the tender pupa and could not resist his urge to help. He went and got a tender pair of forceps to help the egg break, a nip here and a nip there to help the struggling life. The pupa was out and the man was excited with his achievement. He now waited each day for the pupa to grow and fly like a beautiful butterfly. But unfortunately it never happened, the larvae pupa had an oversized head and kept crawling along in the pot for full 4 weeks and died. Depressed the man went to his botanist friend and asked him the reason. His friend told him that the struggle to break out of the egg helps the larvae to send blood to the wings and the head push helps the head to remain small so that the tender wings can support it thru its 4 week life cycle. In his eagerness to help the man destroyed a beautiful life. This shows that struggles help us, that is why a wee bit of effort goes a long way to develop our strength to face the problems in our life. As parents sometimes we go too far to protect our kids from life's harsh realities and disappointments. We feel that our kids should not struggle like we did. But Harvard psychiatrist Dr Dan Kindlon says that over protected children are more likely to struggle in relationships and with facing challenges. By doing so we are sending the kids the message that they are not capable of helping themselves. It is our Job to prepare our children for the road and not prepare the road for our children." I am sure this one example so beautifully illustrates the importance of balanced upbringing and the importance of proper guidance to the kids during their formative years.

How we treat our kids and what we teach them, how we behave with them and the environment they grow up in plays a big role in how they behave and how they grow up. We can see for ourselves if we are attentive and ready to analyze, how we behave in our day to day lives and see how the kids are behaving.

It will be seen that if your child lies to you often, it is because you over reacted too harshly to something they had done or said. If we do not teach our child to confide in us then we will find that we have lost them. They will not share things and try to hide things which they feel may result in the parents scolding them or treating them harshly.

If the child has poor self esteem, it is because we advice and instruct them, in fact dictate them more than we encourage them. Dictating the kids all the time and telling them what to do, will reduce their ability to take decisions and always make them dependent on others to take the risks. They will find it very difficult to lead.

If the child does not stand up for themselves, it could be because we have disciplined them regularly in front of others from a young age. These kids when they grow up will mostly accept what they are being told, without challenging something even if they know it is not right. They will at best be yes man.

If the child takes things that do not belong to them, it is because when we buy things we do not let them choose what they want. We tell them what they need. This lack of choice may force the kid to try to get things which they like by other means.

They develop a feeling that if they ask for something what they want, they are not going to get it.

If the child is cowardly or has lack of confidence it could be because we have helped them too quickly and have not allowed them to find a solution for themselves. Unless the kids are allowed to struggle to find a way for themselves and make mistakes they will not develop the ability to take risks and make decisions.

This is also demonstrated by the story about the gardener which also showed that it is the little struggles early on what prepares the child for facing challenges later on in life.

If the child does not respect other people and their feelings it is because instead of speaking to them and trying to understand them and guiding them, we order and command the child. We are not ready to give time to find out what is it that has made the child behave in this way. Giving them time and explaining them would have a much more positive and lasting effect on how the kid behaves in the future.

If the child has a short temper and gets angry quickly it could be seen that as parents we give too much attention to their misbehavior and give too little attention to their good deeds and behavior and do not encourage them for the same. It could be that these kids have seen that they get attention more easily and quickly when they cry or throw some tantrums rather than asking for something from their parents. With the passage of time this becomes a habit.

If the child is very jealous, it is because it will be seen that the parents only congratulate them only when they successfully complete something and not when they improve at something even if maybe they have not been able to complete something as we had wished.

If the child seeks attention all the time and physically disturbs you it could be that we as parents are not physically affectionate enough or maybe we love them but they feel the lack of affection.

If the child is openly defiant it could be because the parents threaten to do something but actually do not follow through. Threatening a child every time and in fact not going through with will give the impression that no matter what they do finally nothing will happen. It is always better to sit with the child and try to explain things rather than give him empty threats.

If the child talks back to his parents for sure they watch their parents do it to others and their elders and so think that it is a normal behavior. When the child see that every day their parents are quarreling or misbehaving with each other, they start to feel that it is normal way of behaving when you do not like something or when things do not happen as his liking.

If the child rebels it is for the reason that they know and see regularly that parents care more about what others think than what is right or wrong. The tendency to bow down to opinion of the others is very harmful to the parents and the kids. There is no end to what you will have to do what you will demand from the kids so that you can just show to others.

It is often seen that kids that are secretive are those whose parents blow things out of proportion. They had seen from previous experience that instead of guiding them and listening to their point of view the parents just make a scene and berate the kids. The kid feels that best thing to do and keep out of trouble is to hide things from their parents. The less they know better it is as it will save him the trouble of getting on the wrong side with his parents.

Take the small example of teaching the kid from the beginning to wash his hands before he sits in the table to have his food. Is a domestic help going to ever tell this to the kid. It is a very simple thing but a very important habit as it will keep a lot of germs away and prevent a lot of diseases. We all must be remembering swine flu disease which had played havoc in not so distant past, the main recommendation of doctors was to keep washing you hands after shorter intervals. A person who has developed the habit of washing his hands properly before eating anything has at least 50% less chance of contracting the disease just because he will wash his hands at least 4-5 times a day naturally as he has been doing this since the early years.

Now let us look at the case of a kid who has been taught by his parents to be tolerant, well mannered and respect fellow human beings against one who has seen his father who is brash and ready to fight at the first instance of provocation. In western countries when there is a road accident the condition of the vehicle permitting people take their vehicles to the side, inform police and wait for insurance and law to take its due course. In our case depending on which part of the country the accident has happened it may lead to an altercation or in extreme cases physical assault wherein cases of severe injury to death can result. In a city like Delhi it is always a great threat and hassle if you happen to be in a situation where you have accidentally hit another car or maybe another person has hit your car due to the culture that has developed over a period of time where people assume that might is right. People always take things into their own hands and it does not matter who is at fault. The one who has might is always right. At the drop of hat people are ready to physically assault each other without caring for law and police to come and handle the situation. The way the person involved in the accident will behave depends a lot on the way he has seen his parent or elders behave when he was a kid. I was amazed while speaking about kids to a person I know. He is from Delhi and while casually talking it came out he was very much worried about his son, who is not very serious about his studies though his examination is coming very near, that too Board examination for class 12th. He returns late and spends a lot of time with his friends not giving the upcoming career determining exam also too much importance. While talking more, it came up that his son drives his car though he is still not 18 and does not have a learner's license also. When I asked him how the parents are allowing him to drive I was told that it is very difficult to stop the kid when many of his classmates even take car to the school by themselves and it has become like acceptable that kids are allowed to drive without proper license. By allowing the kids to drive a car without a license, not only the parents are putting their kids at big risk but also putting other lives in danger, as there is a reason why someone is not eligible for license before 18 and has to go through the process of getting a learner's license first before he gets a proper driving license that permits him or her to drive on own. Here it is not the kids but the parents who are at fault as they have not been able to educate their kids that they should not drive unless they reach the right age and have the proper document. The father and mother both have taken the easy way out of accepting that since other kids are doing how they can stop their son from driving a car. By allowing the kids to drive a car like this besides putting them at risks, they have also indirectly encouraged the kids to think that it is all right if you do not respect the law.

How parents can educate their kids and inculcate long lasting habits in their kid is very well illustrated in the following conversation with a friend of mine who had just returned from the States where he was for a month with his family. He was staying there with his sister's family who had immigrated there long time back. The kids were born and brought up there and have studied there only. He was there in the month of Ramadan which is a holy month for the Muslims wherein they keep fast from sunrise to sunset. He has also a kid who has grown up in Dhaka, Bangladesh. He never used to do fasting here and used to tell his parents that it is not possible for him. After staying in

US with his cousins and seeing them fast every day, this kid also started fasting from the fifth day and did it continuously for the next 25 days without complaining even once. I am sure this kid will continue doing fast during the Ramadan from now on through the rest of his life. This is a very good example of what influence parents can have on the kids in their formative years. The parents of the kids who were born and brought up in US had definitely been able to inspire and educate their kids about the values and importance of fasting during the holy month staying in a foreign country.

Another very good example he gave was still more interesting. The kids of his sister used to duly do all their school and college work and then come to join the family for dinner and then sit with the family for exchanging thoughts and general talking. Before going to bed they used to keep all the shoes lying outside in the shoe rack. My friend said that after 3-4 days he saw his kids not only keep their shoes in proper place but helped the cousins in putting the other shoes also in the shoe rack. During the weekend all the kids joined together to mow the lawn and also clean the cars, which definitely they had never done here in Dhaka. On hearing the above I became a little more curious and asked him how could the parents cultivate such habits in their kids, both being working parents and being in a country like States. He told that both the parents were very clear that to bring up the kids with values they have to give proper time and guidance to the kids. So when the kids were growing up the father being an engineer always used to work in the night shift and be available for the kids during the day when the mother used to be away on her job. He also had to let go of a few promotions so that he could continue to be with the kids when they were growing up. Maybe in this competitive world all of us may not be able to duplicate such sacrifice but the example shows that when there is a will there is always a way to give time to the kids and it has a huge impact on the upbringing of the kids and goes a long way into making them much better citizens.

The child in his young age is very much influenced by what he sees from his parents and what he is taught by his parents at home. In fact the father is the hero for any son and similar is the story of the mother for her daughter. I was born in a family where both my parents were teachers. So maybe naturally I got the habit of certain respect for teachers. But I had seen many parents criticize the teachers of their kids in the presence of the kids. In extreme cases I have seen parents arguing with teachers for 1 or 2 marks which they feel the teacher should have given to their kids. What a kid who sees all this will learn from his parents, for him disrespecting his teacher will come very naturally. A child who has not learnt to respect his teacher may score good marks with the continuous involvement of the parents at home or by going to private tutorials after school but for sure he will not be an educated man.

Another example which will illustrate how the parents influence their kids, comes from own personal life. It was maybe when I was studying in school and maybe 17 years old. My father had by then become a principal in the school. The Central School that time was very much sought after school especially for the non Assamese students. One evening a person came to meet my father and was discussing about admission for his two kids. My father was explaining to him that it was very difficult for civilian kids to get into the school as it was basically for kids of the armed forces and then next preference would be for kids of central government employees who are on transferable jobs. Only if any seat is left vacant then there is an entrance test and whoever scores the highest marks gets the vacant seats. Then this person said that he had come with great hope and in fact he had bought Rs 100,000 for each of the kids. He said my father could keep it anyway, he had very well understood the procedure but just incase any opportunity comes even after 1 year his kids maybe considered. My father used to earn maybe Rs 10,000 at that moment, and Rs 200,000 would have been very tempting for him but due to his principles he refused to take the money. This incident made me realize that how you earn your money is more important than how much money you earn. I can say with pride that it has stayed with me till now.

With the world changing at a very rapid pace and the coming of internet and social networking the role of parents is becoming still more important in the proper guidance and development of young child. The emergence of internet has broken down all boundaries and everything is available at the click of mouse to a child. Kids have their own Facebook identities where they are communicating with known and unknown people. It is very important for the parents to monitor what the kids are looking at the internet, because today's kids are very curious and there is no limit to what they can be exposed to on the internet. Used in a diligent way internet can be a boon as a lot of information is available on the net which can be used to learn more. At the click of mouse Google can give a lot of information which may have required to go to a library and searching a lot of books to get earlier. But at the same time left to a child without monitoring, internet also has adult and porn sites where anyone can say he is 18+ and enter. There is every chance of a kid getting addicted into these sites once he starts accessing them which could derail a kid and shift his total focus.

It is very important that parents monitor the use of internet by child specially when he is at a young age and also guide them how to use the internet in a positive way.

Today kids as young as 11/12 years have their own Facebook account and making friends. The world is at their doorstep, they are free to come in contact with anyone in the globe who also has a Facebook account. I have heard cases where kids as young as 12 years have made comments about their female classmates in degrading way on their Facebook page. There are cases where a girl has given her mobile no in her Facebook page and have been harassed later on by calls from know and unknown people. Some kids goes to the extent of updating their every movement on the Face book making their whole life public to the entire world putting them at grave risk (in fact a lot of adults also are guilty to this). It is very important for the parents to educate the child on the risks of using social networking sites, what information to share and also monitor the Facebook accounts till a certain age until the child is mentally grown enough to use it in a responsible way. In today's age it will be a folly for parents to think that they can restrict their kids from using internet so what is important is to monitor the way they are using it and guide them so that they learn how to use it in a responsible way.

A lot of the crimes involving teenagers and youths that happens these days is not only because of poverty but because of the families to which the kids belong. If poverty would be the reason for the kids taking to crime all kids of poor families would be criminals and there would not be any crimes committed by the kids who come from middle and rich class families. On careful examination it would be found that most of the kids who take to crime at an early age come from families where they have not been given proper attention by the parents. It could be because the parents are separated putting too much pressure on single parent or the parents may be staying together but are so busy with their own work and social engagements that they hardly get to know their child properly making the kids feeling alienated and the kids have never been taught anything about good values and principles in life. Parental love and attention to the needs of the kids and spending of quality time and support & understanding when required is the most important thing during the formative years of the child and go a very long way in shaping the future of the child.

No amount of money and outside help can replace what parents can give to the child and it should be properly understood by all the parents. In many cases fathers may feel that I am the bread earner, I have the right to relax a bit after a hard day work and anyway mother is always there to take care of the child, but the child need time from both the parents as he learns different things from his mother and his father. I was listening to Michelle Obama the first lady in one of the Democratic Conventions for re election of the President. At that time she had a higher popularity rating among the Americans than Mr Obama and Mr Romney. She said he had married her husband because he had the same family values like her and that one reason she was very apprehensive about Mr Obama becoming President was that she and the kids would be deprived of his love and guidance. The statement which touched the hearts of the people and made them feel their first lady was still one of them was "Our parents did not have much to give to us in terms of money but they gave us unconditional Love"

<u>SCHOOLING</u>

Like parents schools have a very important role to play in grooming the kids and show them the right way to enable make them better and responsible citizens. But we have to introspect are the schools doing justice to all round grooming of the kids. It seems in most of the cases it finally comes on the shoulders of the parents to look after the academic requirement of the kids. The whole teaching system seems to be more inclined to the literary aspect of providing education. Few years back we decided to move our son to India as I was working in Dhaka and studying here he would not be able to cope or compete with kids studying in India once he grows up. I went to a well known and premier school in Bangalore as was looking for admission of my son and on enquiring what other activities the school has beside studies was informed that the school only concentrates on literary aspects and if I was looking for all round development of the kid it may not be the right choice. So are these schools trying to make robots of knowledge or even worse burdening the kids with books which they will read but will not be educated in real terms. In today's world we need education which helps in developing the all- round personality so that when these kids become adults they can face the world with confidence.

In general the kids have a syllabus and the teachers try to complete the syllabus during the course of the year based on which students appear for examination during different time of the year and judged based on what they have written during the exam. In most of the schools the way of communication and teaching in schools is like a monologue where the teacher speaks and the students listen to what has been spoken. It is up to the kids to pick up as much as they can what has been taught in the class. As a whole the Indian education system is very hard on the kids and not much importance is given to the feelings, opinions or ambition of the kids leave alone trying to see what special talent a kid has. There is a lot of pressure on the kids who do not perform well academically both in the schools and from the parents. These days projects are given to the kids from time to time but in most of the cases it is burden on the kids and mostly on the parents as they have to be more involved in ensuring that the projects are somehow completed so that the kids can submit the same to their teachers. Usually there is no effort to see whether the projects are adding value to the learning of the kids and there is not much guidance from schools on how to go about doing these projects. What about a kid who has a better inclination say for music, art or sports as compared to literary excellence. Our educational system has failed to evolve to take care of special needs and inclinations of kids other than literary excellence. These extra curricular activities have to be taken care of by the parents by engaging the kids in special classes after the school hours. So the kids are under tremendous pressure to cope up with the pressure of regular school studies along with the other activities which the parents put them into. In most of the cases the stress is always on doing well in the academics as this is the only guarantee to earn a decent living once a kid steps into the real world. Yes exceptions are always there where a kid does well in sports or music along with continuing to excel in academics but exceptions are not we are discussing here. Again something to look at is the way education is imparted to kids in the school. It needs to be seen and analyzed how much of it is practical and will actually help the kids later on with his life. I take for example the subject of Hindi or any other regional language which is taught say till class 10ᵗʰ as a compulsory subject. There is no doubt that every kid should have working knowledge of the national language and it is a very shameful if he has to say that I cannot read or write in my national language, but is it necessary to burden the kids with say literary work of poets and writers, difficult grammatical knowledge or knowing five other words which has the same meaning like say water. In today's world of specialization a lot of general knowledge which cannot be put into much practical use is of no use.

It does nothing much to the development of the kids except for putting extra burden on them, they just try to mug it up for writing the exam as scoring less in this subject will affect their final result. The way schools deal with our kids with attention to only academics and that too mostly in a way where focus is on scoring good marks at the exams without sometimes understanding has to evolve sooner than later. The system of education lays a lot of stress on memorizing, which is not bad in some cases like multiplication tables but in general it does not help too much in actual education of the kid. Since the focus is on scoring good marks in the exam the kids and parents put all their energy in memorizing what is in the books and write their exams and mostly forget most of it once the exams are over. There is too much stress on the exams from a very early age. My son studies in class six and I see that he has exams the whole year round. His academic session started in the month of May and he had his first tests in the month in July, the other day I was talking to my wife and she said she is very busy as she has to teach my son as he was having exams, this again in the month of September. I asked her for how many days and she said will continue for around two 2 weeks. I was a little surprised as my son had 5 major subjects and 2/3 minor subjects and so enquired how come exams would go on for so long, and then was informed that between every examination they had one day gap so that the kids could study properly, meaning they could memorize the things. I failed to understand why a kid studying in class six needs one day gap for preparation that too for a mid term exam if he is taught properly at school and the system is geared to teach students in a way where they understand what they have been taught rather than memorize a day before the exam which will serve no other purpose other than scoring good marks at the exam. Since I was talking on the Skype and did not have to worry about my phone bill, I jokingly asked my wife so when is our son having his next exam, and to my surprise she told it will be in the month of Nov. The session gets over in the month on April and for sure he has a final examination, God knows he may have one more exam between Nov to April.

Recently we have changed the school of our son and put him in a school which specializes and takes pride in the fact they prepare the kids for IIT and other entrance exams without the kids having to go for outside coaching classes to prepare for the these entrance tests. The grooming starts from class VI or VII. Every week my son has to take tests based on what he had studied which prepares him for appearing in the entrance exam after he does his 12th Standard. Though the kids have to spend longer hours in school as compared to kids from other schools and initially kids find it difficult as they have to appear in tests every week, it seems for any above average student once he does it for one or two years it become a routine thing for them and will take away the fear of appearing in the exam and will become a natural thing like doing any other normal activity. At the same time since questions are not direct but derived from what kids have been taught kids have to really understand what they have been taught to answer the paper. The most important thing is you do not have to send your kids separately for tuitions after the school. This is the biggest headache for parents once the kids grow and reach higher classes. In any big city traveling is a big headache and imagine kids again spending 2-3 hours for private tuitions after school. If you add the traveling time it could be another 3-4 hours after the school, so where does the kids get time to do anything else apart from studies if they really want to get into a professional course or into any good college after completing the schooling. This I am sure will definitely have an effect on the all round development of the kids. Also these private tuitions do not come cheap. Coaching in good tutorial classes can make a good dent on the pocket of the parents.

So parents are spending first for the schools and then separately for the private tuitions. In a country like India what percentage of parents can afford this kind of money if schools do not impart acceptable level of education to the kids. So definitely there is a big disadvantage for even good students who come from families that cannot afford to spend separately on private tutorials of their kids.

I came to know while talking to a few people whose kids were studying in the USA that when a kid enters a school it becomes the schools responsibility to judge a kid and guide him so that he can utilize his potential to the maximum. It is another thing that they have the problem of abundance and so the kids do not utilize the facilities as for them it is so easy to get. The kids are encouraged to take up their favorite sports, hobbies and proper facilities and guidance is available so that the kids can pursue the same. The students join special activities like soccer club, mathematics club, music club and these activities are pursued within the total time spent by the kids in the school. So no extra burden on the kids or the parents especially to first understand their son/daughter is good in what other areas apart from studies and then find a place where they can take their kids to pursue his or her passion or hobby. In high school the students can choose from a list of courses, which enables the students to have the option of having exposure to a variety of subjects. This opens the mind of the students and they are aware from a much earlier age about what could be the different career options. Besides the regular subjects that are taught to the kids there are elective subjects available with focus on various specialties. Computer as an elective subject will have Word Processing, Graphic Design, Programming, etc. On the other hand Performing Arts will have options of art, ceramics, photography, dance, choir, etc. Another elective subject like Career & Technical education have options like Agriculture, Business, Health Occupation, Journalism, and so on.

With an education system which puts so much pressure on studies and doing well academically and schools where the kids spend 8 hours of their day hardly having facilities as well as encouragement for any other activity other than their basic studies how do we expect to have athletes who will compete with athletes of country like America and win gold medals competing in the Olympics. When the Olympic tournament was going on and we were watching television over a glass of drink a friend of mine commented that it is a shame that a country of 1.2 billion did not win a single gold medal. We won six medals in 2012 Olympics and looking at the schooling system which is so biased towards academics I think the athletes from India have done very well. To excel in any field in the international arena you have to start the basic preparation from a very early age, which definitely has to be when a kid is in school. If you look at the winners of the medals in Olympics it will be seen that they have excelled because of their individual efforts combined with the efforts of parents and coaches rather than being the product of a system which encourages sports or provides a platform for kids to take up sports as a possible way of earning a living and competing in international stage. A very good example could be the case of hockey where India earlier won 8 gold medals in the Olympics. This was during the time when the other nations had not taken to hockey so seriously as a sport. Once the synthetic turf came into place and European nations and Australia started to put into practice better and improved technical training, India have never been able to catch up with these nations. In the 2012 Olympics India could not win a single match during the entire tournament. Maybe we will not be able to emulate the Chinese formula where they identify kids at a very small stage and train them to be winners in the international sports, but definitely due importance to sports with facilities in schools and colleges will go a long way in having sportsmen who can compete in the international stage.

As mentioned earlier a lot of kids do pursue other activities like some sports, music, dance, etc with their own efforts and with the efforts of parents who have to take out time to take the kids to the special classes. Here again if both parents are working it becomes quite difficult and they have to make some special arrangements so that the child is able to pursue these activities. Now when this is also not possible there will be many cases where the kid may have talent but does not get the scope to go any further. It is very essential that as a whole the prevailing education system is looked into and when kids spend so much time in the schools they should have the option of pursuing other activities of their interest apart from academics in the schools. For this not only the schools should have special periods allocated to them but ensure that proper people are available who can give proper training in each such activity. It may be that schools in India may not be able to provide such a wide range of extra curricular activities like in schools abroad but definitely there has to be at least a choice of some activities from which students can choose and may select as one of their career options also going forward. It is not that schools abroad which offer these facilities are private schools taking huge amount of money to offer these facilities. In fact in America these facilities are available in all public schools where schooling is free for the kids.

I have been discussing till now the schooling system in general and have taken good schools in bigger cities. If we go a little further down to the schools run by Government aid where education is much cheaper and runs on funding by the State or Central Government the situation deteriorates as these schools have lesser facilities and in some cases teachers are not available as required and also cases where teachers are available but do not take their classes regularly. If we go down to the countryside then schools are there in many cases just for the name of it. There are no proper rooms, students study in make shift classrooms and there will not be enough teachers and even if there are teachers they maybe coming to schools mostly for collecting their monthly salaries. In a country where still 70% of the population still resides in the villages if basic education of schooling is not available to the kids, definitely the country has a long way to go before we can come anywhere near the more developed nations in the globe. I very well remember the elections of 2004 where the ruling party BJP had brought the elections forward to cash in on their perceived thought of popular support with their slogan of India Shining, but were surprised to loose the elections due to mostly losing in the countryside which had not seen any of the signs of the country shining on which the party was banking on to come back to power. In fact their whole campaign with advertisement of the country shining in television backfired when people in the villages saw they have not been benefited in any way from the development and felt cheated by the whole campaign of India shining.

The Central and the State Education Boards has to play a very big role in the education system in the country. Of course these education boards depend on funding from the respective governments running the states and from the centre. For one the private schools cannot cover the entire population and secondly they will come up only where it is economically viable. Unless the government works with all their sincere efforts towards this end education for all will remain only in dreams for generations to come. What is being provided as education by most of the government funded schools especially in the countryside is a big joke. Yes in a country like India there are many things which the government is expected to do and the budget available is not sufficient to take care of all the requirements, but this is where sincerity of efforts and prioritizing has to play a very big role in deciding how and where to spend the money that the government has at its disposal at the start of every year when they are doing the budgeting. India spends 65% of budget on non plan expenditure of which 33% goes to interest and debt servicing and 20% on defense and 20% on subsidies. Basically the money to subsidize oil has to be borrowed which accrues interest on it and then paying up that interest eats up a big portion of the money that could otherwise be used for productive purposes. Another big spending is defense , agreed that India having fought wars with both Pakistan and China has to be ready for any external threat, but it is to be seen sincerely if we require to spend such a big portion of our budget on defense and also if the funds are been used properly and how much of it can be reduced by preventing misuse of funds in different ways. There is a lot of scope to reduce the non- planned expenditure by looking at defense, and subsidies (which then increases the borrowing and eventually increased outflow in terms of debt and interest servicing). These funds can later be diverted to productive expenditure like education and infrastructure. Just to take the case of our national airline carrier, it has been years since it has been incurring losses and running on money given by the government. There was a time when it was necessary to run the national air carrier, but now with private airlines covering more and more routes, do not see any point of government running a loss making airlines when there is no sign of the airlines to turn in around in the foreseeable future. Sooner or later someone has to think practically and be bold enough to say that government cannot afford to run a company which does not have any strategic importance and at the same time will only be a drain to the resources of the country, has to be closed or privatized so that the money required to keep it running can be used for things which are essential and has much more productive use.

As it is government allocation for the purpose of education is approx 4.1% of the GDP of the country which is not very small. What is to be seen is how this is been actually used. How much of this is being put into productive use and how much is going to fill in the coffers of the politicians and bureaucrats. There are many cases when state governments are not able to utilize the budgets allocated to them either due to lack of planning or very late release of the funds. One thing is for sure there is a big scope of improvement in terms of both utilization of the allocated funds as well as finding ways to allocate more funds for the purpose of education. As of now the picture is grim with 25% illiterate, of what we call literate, 15% go to high school and of this only 7% go on to graduate. If we want that the country should progress as a whole and we really think of utilizing our population in a constructive way there is a long way to go in terms of first being able to provide just the basic education.

One does not have to be very educated or knowledgeable to know that poverty and, illiteracy is the breeding ground of most of the evils in the society. When there is a situation where kids who go on to become youths do not see any future for them they are driven easily towards all sorts of crime like drug trafficking, stealing, robbery and also drives them into the hands of terrorist and underground organizations. Poverty and lack of opportunities make these people feel that they can find a purpose to their life by joining these groups and lack of education makes it very easy to brain wash these people and be exploited by the leaders of the anti social organizations and groups. Education gives people the power to think and use their brain which in turn enables people to reason with themselves so making it much more difficult for the kids or youth to be exploited easily. If we look at India the naxalite problem is most prevalent in the backward areas of Orissa, Bihar, Andhra Pradesh and Madhya Pradesh. The most fertile breeding ground for the recruits of the terrorist are backward regions of Afghanistan, Pakistan, Yemen, Somalia and similar other countries. So it is time for whoever is in power to have a hard look at how to improve the situation in terms of providing education. It has to start from first ensuring basic education for all the kids, education where the kids just learn to write the alphabets and read a bit to be termed a so called literate will not be of much use. Facility and environment should be created so that more and more kids do at least high school, and the schools specially in the country side has to be improved so that there is availability of teachers and basic infrastructure so that kids feel encouraged to go to the schools.

This will at first help to bring the whole population to a basic level where kids can think in a more constructive way. At the same time for the kids who are interested in studies the schools run by state and central government should have the infrastructure like laboratories, playgrounds, minimum student to teacher ratio and also proper trained staff.

To attract better talent to the teaching profession it may be required to look at the salary structure of the teaching staff. Finally there is a requirement to look at the whole system of education which puts so much load and burden on the kids from a very young age, make the teaching more interactive than just monologue and also due importance and facilities should be given to kids to pursue in school other activities like sports, music, career knowledge, etc so that schools become self sufficient to the all round development of kids rather than be able to pursue only academic interest and that too where such a big stress is on memorizing rather than understanding and assimilating.

Also if we try to analyzc wc will find that the whole education system is geared towards making kids ready for doing a job after completing their schooling and college. Have anyone tried to think that there will be no jobs if there are no entrepreneurs who sets up businesses and make big manufacturing plants. Is it now high time that we think about how to incorporate in our education system, ways to help entrepreneur development. It will be seen that it is usually the small businesses that on the whole creates maximum employment generation and plays a very important role on the overall development of any country. These are the centers that are the breeding places for most of the new innovations and ideas that changes the life of the entire generation. If the country has to progress and create employment for its people, it needs the growth of private enterprises and so due importance should be given to see how to impart education starting from schools that will lead to entrepreneur development, as they are the engines on which the train of growth of the nation will depend.

COLLEGE & HIGHER EDUCATION

As much as schools are the building base for the kids, it is the colleges that they can enter after completion of their studies which plays a very big role in the future career of the millions of graduates who come out every year and become part of the workforce on which depends the future of the country in general and the individuals in particular.

As discussed earlier parents put their child into coaching classes from 8th standard to enable them get into one of the premier Engineering or medical colleges. So the focus is not on learning but preparing for clearing the entrance exams. The lucky few get into the good institutions like IIT's or one of the top medical colleges. For those who cannot get into the good engineering or medical college there are private colleges where more than merit, donation is more important criteria or in some cases influence of a board member or a politician. What the students actually learn in most of these colleges is a big question mark. A field of study that has become very much in demand is MBA with every person wanting to get an MBA degree assuming that it can be the passport to having a good job which can make them earn a lot of money. So these days one can find mushrooming of colleges imparting education in Business Management in all parts of the countries. Just a recent survey I came across in a leading daily showed that the industry found that only 25% of management graduates that pass out from the various Management colleges are actually employable. Nothing to be surprised about as most of the private institutions which claim to be imparting management education are not fit to exist as centre of education. They neither have the adequate teaching faculty nor the necessary tools to give proper education.

I am first taking up the business management graduates as it is one of the most over hyped of courses in the country. Even the bright graduates coming out of the IIT's instead of going for higher studies in their field of study or going for a job in their related field of education want to go for a Management degree. Now why do these graduates who have done their Engineering from the best institutes in the country after preparing to get into the colleges for 3-4 years slogging it out from class 8 or 9 go for management study. This way they are not only diverting from what they learned for 4 years but also deprived another person who could have been very interested in pursuing his career in the engineering or technical field, thereby society would have got two talented person doing well in two different fields as anyone who can get into an IIT or an IIM has definitely above average IQ. Even the companies who come to recruit students from these colleges do not go there for what they have learned but idea is to get a talented pool of people who has higher potential and intelligence than the average students studying in lesser known institutions. The basic idea in most of the cases into getting into an IIT is not the love for learning Engineering, it seems but maybe ensuring that it could be the ticket to a good living and earning in the future. It is the same logic which make these students go for MBA after IIT, not that they suddenly have a dislike for science or engineering and now want to learn business or management. They go for MBA because they know it will increase their market value and will help them to earn a even fatter package. In most cases the pursuit for education is to get a ticket to a rich lifestyle with a lot of money. It has been hammered into the kids from the early age by the parents, the peer pressure and the media which plays a very important role in our lives these days.

Here I have to get a little personal as it is these things which I have experienced myself that motivated me to write. I myself got into an engineering college somehow as like all middle class parents my parents specially my father wanted me to be either a doctor or engineer not because I had a passion for this line of study. Anyways there is no similarity between the studies in a medical and engineering college so logically cannot be either/ or for the love of it but as per them it was the way to success meaning earning a decent package and lead a good life after completion of my studies as that time in the late 80s and early 90s these two were the two coveted professions and ticket to sure shot success in life though in practical life I used to see a lot of engineers without jobs even after 2 years of their passing out from engineering college. In fact my father was standing out of the medical college on the day of admission though I had categorically told him that medical science is not my cup of tea. Then when he did not see me he called up mother and communicated his disappointment when it was clear that I was at home instead of the line of students who were there for admission. By the way my name was at number three in the admission list in Asaam as admission that time in Assam in medical colleges was on basis of your score in class 12 examination. I was in the meantime waiting for the results of entrance examination for getting into an Engineering college. Those days there used to be one or two reserved seats in some Engineering colleges for branch of studies which was not available in the Engineering colleges in Assam and admission to those were based on the percentage of marks scored in the subjects of Physics, Chemistry and Mathematics in the 12th Board examination. I got the choice of doing a course in Textiles in one of the better colleges that imparted Engineering in Textiles. Though I had also cleared the entrance examination for Engineering colleges in Assam which had only the traditional branches of study like Electrical / Mechanical/Civil and few seats for Electronics which were taken by the top rankers in the admission tests I decided to join the college for Textile engineering.

The logic being textile is the biggest employment generator and so at least I will not have to sit at home after completion of four years of studies. Life in hostel was good, in fact the best period of my life, where we used to have a lot of fun. Once you complete your studies like most people one gets busy after they enter the profession and start a job. In most of the cases people spend their lives worrying and running after all mundane things like career, climbing the corporate ladder, marrying and then have kids, buying a house to live in, then career of the child and then also save enough to carry you through the old age. So when I look back I always find the years that I spent in the hostel the best period of my life.

Coming back to the main point of education I can say that the four years spent in the college was not of much use in terms of learning in a practical sense. My basic knowledge helped me picking up the things faster when I started working as compared to a person who had not studied textiles, but I sincerely feel that what we learned in four years could have been done in two years if the course was designed more practically or for four years in the college they should have made it much more elaborate with stress on practical demonstration which could have been much more useful. I could hardly understand why I had to do all the mathematics till two years for learning textiles. Except for one or two teachers who were really good rest of the faculty were either not interested in teaching job except for as a means to livelihood or did not have the right approach to teaching. So slowly I started to attend classes of only those two teachers and for the rest just ensured I had enough attendance to appear in my final exam. There was hardly any machinery where it could be practically demonstrated how actually the things work, whatever was there was obsolete maybe 20 years back. Learning was basically making some notes, collect the notes of the senior batches and somehow mug up whatever necessary to vomit it out during writing the answers and forget about it once you are out of the examination hall and then prepare for the next paper. Still I used to score marks among the top 25 percent students in the class. My parents used to ask me how much I have scored and used to be happy that their son is doing well in his studies. In the third year of my engineering college I saw some of my fellow students starting to prepare for MBA and some for GRE to go to the USA for higher studies in textiles. Since I had not learnt much in terms of textiles so I though no point in wasting further time in trying to learn more about textiles so let me prepare for my MBA. I had heard that the combination of engineering and MBA will land me a good job and at the same I would be able to avoid the initial tough time of working in shifts after completion of my final year. Luckily I got into a college for MBA after clearing my entrance and then going through group discussion and personal interview. Also Management was something which was something more closer to what I would like to do later on as a professional. So I joined the college with a lot of enthusiasm and hope, happy that I would have the right combination of degrees in Engineering and Business Management that would enable me to land up a good job and progress fast in my professional career.

Also I felt I would get more interest while studying as it would be closer to humanities and not technical as in the case of Engineering. I was quite happy after attending the first two classes which were taken by two very good teachers, but very soon realized that they were the best faculty in the college. Apart from these two faculty the other teachers who were taking classes for subjects like marketing, finance, etc were not as good. Their deliberation was monotonous and to sit through their classes was a big struggle as they just used to speak out what was written in the books. Again I started to attend only that many classes so that I could be eligible to appear in the examination. Life in hostel was fun and frolic, having parties, playing games and two years went off very fast. What I actually got in terms of education was maybe not at all worthwhile spending two years, with a little effort and concentration this I could have learnt in 10-12 months. As mentioned earlier I was told that combination of engineering with a major in marketing was the in thing and could take me a long way in my career. Time came for campus interview towards the end of the second year but we had hardly 2/3 companies and maybe at the most three or four students were recruited from campus. I did not appear for any of the interviews as there was no company from the Textile sector. I came across an advertisement in paper for Management trainees for one of the premier textile mill and got the interview call but was not selected so after two degrees and spending six years in doing two professional courses I was without a job when left my college. I have to mention here that I was not bad at studies as it is understood in conventional terms, somehow had a good memory and always used to memorize what was written in books with little effort and so used to score good marks in my examination. So I had degrees but hardly much in terms of real education. What I have learnt was on the job and realized that if I could have started earlier say 2-3 years after completion of my schooling then the practical experience would have been much more useful and in real life I would have been ahead by those two/three years.

Being a son of parents both of whom were teachers, and studying in two professional colleges getting admission in both on the basis of so called merit, the colleges if not among the premier colleges were also not at the bottom, definitely well recognized I am sure that there is definitely something wrong in the way education is being imparted in most of our schools and colleges. The personal example I gave above is not linked to any run of the mill private educational college. These are institutes which were among the mid level educational centers if not among the best in the country, so one can very well imagine the education that is being provided by most of these private colleges in various fields and the quality of graduates that come out from these colleges and becomes a part of the workforce every year.

I had been reading a book by the title "THE BLACK SWAN "by Nassim Nicholas Taleb which challenges many of the conventional thoughts and teachings. He talks about the Black Swan which is basically an event which we cannot predict or anticipate but has unthinkable impact on the lives of millions of people like stock market crashes, earthquake, other natural disasters like tsunami or a big cyclone. He takes a look at the disaster of predicting things linked to social science using conventional models of mathematics. The book is very interesting and relevant and looks at the way things happen in everyday life and in business. I for one has found the book more relevant and mind stimulating than all the books that I read on management during my two years in MBA course.

I have been always interested to see how things work practically than what has been written in the books. More than theory what interests me are things like human behavior, why some people are successful while others are not, what is it that keep people going like the politicians who do not want to quit even when they reach the age of 80, and other things related to human beings and their behavior and its impact in the society. I have seen many cases wherein students who do very well in the class and among the toppers do not do very well in their practical life when they start their professional career and on the other hand people who were in general smart but not very good academically do very well when they start their professional career. There are many cases of school drop outs or college drop outs who do exceedingly well and go on to become very successful businessman and who also has brought out the greatest innovations and done greatest inventions which have changed the way human beings lead their life.

Let us take the case of latest stock market crash in 2008 arising from the sub prime home loans that were given in the preceding years creating a bubble which was waiting to go bust. Some of the biggest names in the financial world like Lehman Brothers, Bear Sterns, Meriyll Lynch, etc went bust or had to be bailed out, and gave to what become famous as TOO BIG TO FAIL. These companies along with others like CITI BANK, Bank of America, and numerous other banks and financial institutions are being run by the so called best talent and brightest people available coming from the best management institutes from around the globe. If you think carefully why most of the brightest finance people got sucked into the crisis and could not see what they were getting into and even if they could see were blinded by what others were doing and kept on finding ways to increase their exposure thereby making the problem bigger and bigger. I could not hear a single fund manager or so called big economists saying that not everything was right and there could be a crisis waiting to happen sooner rather than latter. I myself those days had most of my savings in equity based mutual funds which were being handled by fund managers coming out from the best institutes in the country. I was new into investing in mutual funds and had not studied earlier crashes so naive and one among the many following the crowd. Whenever I used to go to meet the people in bank they only used to talk about why I should put all my funds in equity and how the stock market was going to cross 25000 index very soon, if I remember well it had gone up to 21600 and then the BSE index in no time went below 8000, once the crisis started to unravel initially in the United States. Since I had started investing in equity mutual funds when the BSE index was around the level of 8000 my portfolio was still worth 50% of the principal amount that I had put in at different stages. Even at 21000 level my client service manager coaxed me into investing in new funds, I am sure with the best intention and knowledge that the only direction the market knows is to go up.

I remember analysts and financial experts talking of the BSE going up to 30,000 or even 35000 because when the going is good everyone is bullish and not able to see the downside and just want to go with the crowd. When the market started to fall again it was the same, but the other way round. Whoever I used to talk advised that I should cut my losses and come out of the market, but problem was so called experts started to give this expert advise when market was down to say 12000 level and already most of my investments were in the red and overall the portfolio looked horrible. I remember being advised to invest at 15000 level when the market was coming down, the sound argument being market has corrected itself and at these levels I could only expect the market to go up. So I waited and saw the market to go below 8000 and still there were people telling me that I should cut my losses and come out of the market. My wife who never used to interfere in my financial matters told me that what a wrong decision I had taken to invest in mutual funds and loose all the hard earned money.

This is the point when I started reading a bit about the past crashes, and thought I should use my own judgment rather than do what the finance guys in banks tell me to do. I have to tell here that I still do not know much about stocks and markets but still feel it is better to take my own decisions, in this way I will not have to blame someone else or regret for what someone else decided for me. It is the same logic I use when I am on a high way in a car. Even though I have a driver with me I do not allow him to drive as then I am not letting my driver decide my fate by not slowing down and making a split second mistake while driving at a speed of 120 kms/hr.

Luckily I did not need the money immediately and so I decided to keep invested with the thought that when I am already more than 50% down the worst that could happen is I will loose all my money. I had a job and have to start all over again, people have to sometime go through worse than this when there is a war or a natural disaster.

With time the market went started to go up and I started to come out of my investments at different times starting from when index was above 16000 and had gone up to 21300 in 2011.

One of the biggest treat to well being of people leaving in today's age more than natural disaster, war, disease or terrorism is the banking and the financial industry as a whole. In the latest financial meltdown not only did the banks and financial institutions lured people into taking housing loans which they could never repay creating an artificial bubble but made complex derivates based on these risky investments and assets which even the top bosses do not understand. Then these complex and toxic derivates were sold and resold making the whole financial system in the developed world toxic and waiting to come down like a pack of cards sooner rather than later. In the meantime the so called financial wizards coming from best of the management institutes made huge salaries and bonuses at the cost of unknowing public and small investors. Even when governments were using tax payers money to bail out these banks and financial institutions they were continuing to give million dollar salaries and bonus to the top management, the argument being to keep the bright talents in the payroll they have to continue paying else they would not be able to retain them.

Even when the CEO is forced to resign due to his negligence and role in huge financial losses, the bank and financial institutions reward him by giving multi- million dollar package as severance money. The banks which are supposed to protect the money of the investors who put their hard earned money in good faith, gamble with their money putting the whole financial system into risk and then coerce the government into bailing them out as they are too big to fail. With the entire financial system being interconnected with hardly any real time monitoring of the risky deals they do even after the last crisis, I am sure we should not be surprised if sooner rather than later we see another similar situation. Not only this very recently there was the case of HSBC bank having to pay a huge sum as compensation in USA for transactions whereby they had allegedly helped drug cartels in Mexico transfer huge sums of money. The problem is everyone wants to make quick money and more money and there is no limit to how much money one needs.

I find that what is being taught in the colleges and what you actually encounter in practical life is not the same especially in a field like management. What is being taught is based on theories and models which do not take into account the various variables which are beyond control not to mention about variables which we cannot anticipate at all. What is taught in the management colleges is based on theory and it is supplemented by cases studies from actual happenings in different industries, but still do not take into account all the variables which come into play in real world and definitely not the factors which are unseen but can have wide ranging and both dramatic impact in positive and negative sense. Again when the best of the management schools cannot prepare the students for what they are going to encounter in actual life, I just cannot comprehend of what use can be studies in all the private colleges that come in every nook and corner with the motive of earning money as the main motto rather than imparting knowledge. What we were taught in our MBA was mostly what was written in the books and as far as I can remember we were given not more than 2/3 cases per subject in a year, which too were not very relevant when had to face the real world. I feel if one enrolls into one of the MBA courses after he has worked in the real world for 2-3 years at least then with the availability of competent faculty supported by guest visitors from industry it will enable the students to make more sense of what they are studying and relate the theoretical assumptions to practical life. Also this way after they work in the industry for some time they will be better able to select what is the field they should be specializing in like marketing, production, finance instead of going with the crowd and opting for something which the majority is going for. It could be much more useful if the students are motivated to change the thinking process whereby they start to appreciate and take into consideration the impact of known and unknown things which could drastically change the whole equation, take the various social factors into consideration and learn to look at things from bottom to top then from top to bottom. After working for about 20 years in private organizations and having traveled all around the globe I feel management is not a science and does not follow any set principle or theory but more of an art where one has to learn by observation, interaction with people from all levels of the organization, reacting to the prevalent situation without delaying the decisions and appreciate that the human factor is the most important as compared to all other factors which influences how an organization whether it a private company, NGO or any government department operates and gives results. Another very important factor which has to be taught and inculcated is that it is not possible to solve human problems with science, mathematics or any theoretical models. It is something which is to be observed, felt and understood. This human angle is neglected in most of the management institutions which I feel is one of the major reasons why management graduates fail in real life. I was reading this book "The Age of the Unthinkable by Joshua Cooper Ramo where he has given instances of successful people discard the black and white models which they study in their colleges and learn to adopt to different probable situations and scenarios. He has given the example of Henry Kissinger a former Harvard professor while meeting with Zhou Enlai the Chinese leader for establishing China – US relation admitted that many of the ideas they were discussing were almost exactly opposite to the theories he once used to teach.

I have taken up the case of management studies at the beginning as it is the most coveted field of study these days. In reality apart from the premier colleges we should also take into consideration the fact that there are also thousands of graduates who come out of the sub standard so called private management institutes who are not employable in most of the cases or start as basic salesman even doing door to door selling, direct selling or selling over telephone. You do not need to waste two years of your life after graduation spending a lot of money to get a degree where by you do not get any meaningful education to do this kind of a job. Ability to communicate with people in a language which is being spoken in a particular part of the country with a brief training to give the young person knowledge about the product or service they would be selling and a little bit of grooming up will make the person well equipped or even better than what a fresh MBA will be able to do in real world.

Now coming to technical fields like engineering and medical science, here also there are many colleges which impart education to thousands of students after taking huge sums of money, but without proper facilities like laboratories and competent faculty. I had myself experienced this during the four years that I had spent studying in a reputed college doing my engineering as mentioned earlier. That was the time when still education was not so commercialized in the country. But problem was that there was no proper facilities where one could get practical training. Though the college was located in a city where there were many industries in the same field there was no initiative on the part of the teachers or the college management to collaborate with the industry and arrange visit to get practical knowledge which would have made the education more meaningful and at the same time more interesting. I am sure most of the lower level colleges which give engineering degrees to thousands will definitely be much worse than what I had encountered. How can these thousand of engineering students contribute meaningfully to the industry is beyond my comprehension. I was going through an article in an English daily regarding the young and jobless in the north Europe. It was mentioned that even in Belgium which has an open end high tech economy with one of the highest per capita income in the world the unemployment rate among the youths is on the rise. Yes the economy was not very good with most of Europe not doing financially well but as pointed out by a minister maybe very rightly the problem was increased by the fact that the education being offered was not always in tune in what the market needs. At least there someone is accepting and analyzing, which definitely is not the case in our country. Yes we have the biggest young workforce available with us but if it is not in tune with what the industry requires will it be able to contribute with high efficiency that is required to compete with today's competitive world where due to globalization and opening up of markets world is becoming a single market where the survival of the fittest is becoming more a rule than an aberration. In a study conducted by Times of India in partnership with J.P Morgan it was found that of the 13 crore students that enroll in primary schools 11% make it to college. But more importantly for a growing economy like India where skilled workforce is required to run the industry and work in shop floor only 20 lakh students go to Polytechnics and industrial training institutes after finishing school in class X or class XII.

Will it not be worthwhile to have a look at how to utilize the pool of young people that we have in our country. Instead of following the conventional way of imparting education why cannot we think of finding ways to teach people skills so that they can make real contribution to the society and at the same time take care of themselves better. Say for people who want to join the banking industry they should have courses and educational centers which are specialized in giving education and training to people for different functions and departments that exist in the banking industry. It should cover all aspects related to particularly the banking indusrty with due importance to soft skills like how to deal with different kind of clients, imbibe in the people who are at the front end the importance of giving proper service and guidance to people they are dealing with. Maybe people who will handle loans and credits should have some training in psychology so that they can try to understand better who could be a genuine client and who could have some ulterior motives while applying or seeking loans from the bank. Similarly people who have an inclination to work in the hospital and medical care sector should have training institutions where they specialize to train people who will later on work in this sector.

Indian Railways is a vast organization employing lakhs of people who work at different levels and requires different sets of skills. It is still the main mode of transportation for the vast population of the country and also handles a huge volume of goods that are transported within the country. It has one of the widest networks in terms of distance covered and is going to be a vital lifeline for the transportation of goods and people for years to come. I for one still do not see a situation where Indian Railways is going to be privatized and also do not want it to be as privatization may not be good here as beside commercial function, railways has a social function which is always ignored when privatization happens where money making takes the top priority. Why cannot Railways have a training center for the people who want to work in this sector The training center should have proper facilities with competent people who are taken from the railways to give training and education that is related and practical to the needs of the Indian Railways. Maybe it will be much more worthwhile for the people who want to join this sector after completion of their schooling rather than spending three years for their graduation studying something like English literature. These people could be trained for two or three years as per the requirement and the department which they are going to join giving the railways more competent people who will be able to do their job better being specifically trained for what they are going to do.

Now let us look at the colleges and educational institutions which are not offering technical education like engineering, medical, biotechnology, or any other professional course. Here students that enroll for education are mostly those who have not been able to get into a professional course either because they have come short on merit or they have not been able to afford to spend the money required to get into any of the private colleges where it is too costly for a student coming from a normal middle class where parents do not have other sources of income beside what they get as salary at the end of the month.

Except for few good colleges in the big cities, the standard of education in most of the colleges is not up to the level where students will learn much other than getting a degree after spending three years in the college. The teachers in many of the colleges do not go to take their classes and more busy with earning extra money by taking classes in coaching centers and taking private tuitions. This is more true in the case of government funded colleges. Students attitude is no better, they join colleges not as a place for learning but as a medium to get a degree. Some of them go on to become teachers after completion of studies. I wonder what education they will give to students when they themselves have not been educated.

Let us take the case of students learning medicine. In earlier days medical profession was considered as one the noble profession along with teaching. But with the commercialization of education becoming a doctor has also become more a means to making money rather than ensuring that the first priority is to see the patient gets the right treatment and advise. I am of the very strong opinion that in a profession like medical science there should not be any seats reserved on the basis of caste and admissions should solely be on the basis of merit. This is a field of study wherein if students are not given proper education and training in the medical colleges it is very dangerous as they would never be able to do proper diagnosis and will play with the lives of the people who go to them for treatment. It is a profession where there should be proper monitoring of the colleges on a regular basis and those colleges which are not up to the mark should not be allowed to function at all.

The level or quality of education and more so the utility of education specific to a particular job requirement can be illustrated with a very simple example. India used to be the leader in BPO industry till very recently, but has been taken over by Philippines. The medium of education in most of the educational centers whether it is school or college is in most cases either local language or English in our country against the option of Filipino or English in Philippines. Compared to India's population of over 1200 million, Philippines has a population of approx 92 million. With less than 10 times the population of India Philippines has overtaken India in a field where the basic requirement is knowledge of English and ability to handle the queries or requirements of clients who are sitting in US or UK. It is not that Philippines is cheaper, in fact in some cases clients are paying more for shifting their outsourcing to Philippines and also some Indian companies have shifted some of their operations to that country. Combining their natural warmth and friendliness with a neutral and better English speaking capability a small country has overtaken India in BPO business and they expect the gap to widen in the years to come.

It is high time that the whole education system is looked into in a different perspective. There has to be a proper monitoring body independent from the influence of the politicians and government like the Election Commission which will monitor the educational institutions in terms of the availability of the proper faculty, and facilities. The way education is imparted has to be reviewed, it has to be more practical oriented and synchronized with what is required by the market and the industry so that the young graduates who are coming into the work pool can contribute positively and efficiently to the industry in general and the country as a whole.

Educational and professional institutions along with academicians should think and find ways to educate the students on the social side of the business including aspects such as the human factors, how to protect the environment, moral values, understating the probabilistic nature of events, ability of think and use their brains in a constructive way which will then bring into the society a workforce which is more useful, complete and so much more productive. The country needs people who are open to newness, and appreciate the challenges which will be encountered while performing their jobs in a productive and honest manner. Trying to carry fixed notions and ideas and being not flexible should automatically disqualify any person from holding any important position either in the industry or any government or non government organization.

It is very important for tomorrow's leaders whether they are running a government or any industry to appreciate that the best way to bring and sustain growth is by creating the proper environment where people are encouraged to bring in new ideas, there is openness and appreciation for the efforts being put in.

I would like to go a step further here and study what we can do in the direction of developing human resource development and training people in fields and areas which would be an asset for the country and at the same time would be required by countries where there is negative population growth rate for many years now and population is ageing fast. It has to be studied what are the sectors in these countries which would need people from outside to sustain their society and the economy. This way not only will people get opportunity to learn a good livelihood but at the same time contribute to the economy of our country by means of foreign exchange remittance to our country. It could be sectors like education, health care, retailing, construction, etc. where there will be not sufficient people in certain affluent countries in years to come. What is required to develop a pool of people in certain sectors is basically a different line of thinking and initiative from both the government and the private sector. The business owners and entrepreneurs are able to do their business because of the support of the government and society. The government facilitates and creates the environment where people can run their business using tax payers money and so it will not be wrong to expect the business community to contribute a part of their earning to the society by opening up training centers and institutes which will help develop a pool of well trained and educated young people.

IT'S THE PEOPLE WHO MAKE A NATION

It is the young people who have completed their studies in different fields and different levels and come into the work pool that shapes the whole future of the country with their positive or negative contributions. Some finish their studies because of choice as they are more interested in doing productive work that would give them financial independence, some because they had aspirations to study more but could not get through due to other students who were better than them in clearing the tests for the next grade. There are a huge majority who had to leave their education as they could not afford it financially, had to join their parents to supplement their income to run the family and so had to drop out at school or just after completing their school. But no matter up to what level a person has studied each and ever one who joins the productive working pool has a role to play in the overall economy the country. With the opening up of the economy and higher growth rates since the 1990s the opportunities available to youngsters is much more and they also have a lot more freedom in deciding what they want to be in their lives.

But again the education system that they have come through will play a big role in what they contribute, and how they are useful to the industry in general and the society at large.

Let us just look at the influence different professions and people have on the society and how the role they play impacts the country as a whole. Though our country got independence in 1947, in many ways were not able to come out of the influence Britain had due to 200 years they had ruled our country. There is nothing to be embarrassed about this as for a newly independent country the nation leaders had to follow some system which was already working somewhere than trying to do something new and of course it is always easier to implement something which we have been used to. One of the most influential group of people due to following the British system of administration was the IAS officers. They are responsible for the running the country in terms of making policies, running administration, guiding the politicians with facts and first hand information, in fact these people who are being selected every year after a process that involves a preliminary written test where a large portion of the candidates are rejected, followed by a final written tests wherein there is further screening and elimination and then the final interview which is conducted by a panel of experts selected by the Union Public Service Commission. Finally about 850 candidates are selected who occupy key positions in Central government, State governments and Public Sector Undertakings. When I was at school in the 1980s this used to be the most coveted position one could aspire for as a career, which gives prestige, fame and money. For youngsters of certain States sometimes this was like their passport to the future, I had seen students leaving their homes and stay in places like Delhi for years together (as usually you are allowed multiple attempts to clear the 3 stages) to attend coaching classes and prepare for their exam. When I was doing my MBA I had a classmate who had taken admission into MBA just as a back up, but he hardly used to attend the classes. He did not use to stay at hostel with us but stayed in a rented house with 3 other guys who were all preparing for the IAS examination. Getting selected into IAS ensured that they had a secure future with lot of money and helped by increased valuation in the marriage market, and could be the passport to getting a big amount of money as dowry. The basic motive of a lot of these youngsters for appearing is IAS exam is not their desire or interest to serve the people and the ability to shape the future of the country by holding key positions in government and Public sector undertaking, the main motivation is the prestige associated with it, which gives a standing to the whole family in the society, along with ensuring a secure future with the possibility of earning a lot of money due to their position which enables them to do favors to people who have the capability to return the same in cash or kind. I am not saying that everyone is like that but a big majority definitely falls into this category. Also there will be many who start with all the good intention but the system forces them to change after a certain time. The candidates which clear the very tough examination and scrutiny process where finally 850 odd people are selected from over 500,000 candidates who appear for the Preliminary examination every year have to really work hard for years and definitely have to be academically good to come through the entire process. The selected candidates go into various departments like IAS, IRS, IPS and other public sector organizations and departments.

The vital and important thing to ponder about here is whether this is the best way to select the people for the key positions that they would occupy in the bureaucracy and also if these people who have been selected after such a long and comprehensive selection process give the best people to hold the key positions and carry out their responsibilities.

Agreed that the whole screening process enable us to find out the best 850 candidates who have worked the hardest in their studies and have been maybe coached by the best coaching centers in the country. These people must have slogged day and night for 2-3 years, burnt their midnight oil, for sure they had to sacrifice a lot of things including being away from the family, missing festivals, giving a miss to the cricket match or the live performance of their favorite artists to finally get selected among the 850 candidates. But I very much doubt that this selection process can actually find out who could be a good administrator or who could give direction to turn around an sick or loss making Public sector undertaking into a profitable one. Being academically good and ability to work hard to clear a certain examination cannot ensure that they will be good at what they are supposed to do in their actual life.

The argument is that the selection process allows to find out the brightest candidates from all who aspire to be selected. As mentioned earlier I do not agree to this concept as I have seen many students who were very good in scoring good marks in the examination but could not do very well in practical life even in the field which they had done their studies.

Then the process of allocation of the departments has to looked into. The finally selected candidates gets into IAS, IRS, IPS or any of the allied services not because they have been deemed fit for that department but based on the ranking the candidates get in the examination. Mostly their first preference is IAS or IFS, then maybe in the next preference it could be IRS or in some cases IPS. So basically the score obtained in the selection process decides who is going to be good as an IAS/IRS/IPS officer in the years to come. Another very important factor to consider is the basic education of the candidates who has been selected. A candidate who had spent his days in the college say studying Chemistry most of the time either studying books or being in the college laboratory learning about the various reactions of different chemicals, can do very well in the examination and selection process but when he is put into real world in charge of running the district administration he may be a total failure as basically he is an academician.

Again let us take another case where there are two candidates one who has done his post graduation in history/social science and another who has done his studies in commerce. Due to the ranking in the examination the candidate who studied commerce got IAS and went onto become an IPS officer and the candidate who studied social science got into Allied services, so got Indian Railways Accounts Services. Now this is a case wherein the two candidates would be doing things which are different from what they studied, and maybe could have been more useful or a at least given the candidates some head start in their professional career if would have been other way round.

Again there is reservation based on caste for candidates in this very vital area of governance. Agreed that the lower strata of the society which come under categories of Scheduled Castes and Scheduled Tribes had to suffer a lot during earlier days and they need to get facilities to come up in the society, but is reservation at every stage of education and job which can be so vital for the society the way to uplift the people.

An IAS /IPS / IFS officer has a very important role to play in the overall development and administration of the society and the country in general. Putting someone who is not competent enough but has got the post of say administration of a district will do more harm than good to the development of that area. I feel a better way to uplift the people of the lower section of the society is to ensure free education which is of good quality so that the kids from these section can get a chance to study in primary schools and also provide concessions in terms of fees and monetary support to the deserving students so that they can pursue higher education and not have to leave education due to the inability of the poor parents to provide monetary support for pursuing higher education. In this way a larger proportion of the backward class kids will be benefited and in a much shorter period these people can come up in the society. Moreover when they take up a responsible position they will be able to make positive contribution to the society as they will be there because they deserve to be there on their merit not because they got the position due to reservation. In fact it will solve a much bigger problem which the country is facing now. The politicians will no longer be able to divide the country on the basis of caste and creed as they will not be able to play with the sentiments of these people if this reservation is abolished. We will not have politicians who come to power using the division of castes thereby forcing them to really perform and do constructive work without bias towards any particular section of the electorate thereby bringing genuine performers into the corridors of power.

The above logic holds true for every profession. Take the case of doctors who are as in shortage due to restrictions on private universities providing medical courses unlike in the case of engineers and MBAs. Now if a big percentage of the seats available in the medical colleges goes to students based on reservation then definitely the country is loosing out on the overall quality of the doctors that it is getting every year in a field where there is already a big scarcity in the no of doctors available as percentage of the population in the country. This is a profession which is very noble one and at the same time very important one. When a patient goes to a doctor he puts his total faith on the diagnosis and treatment suggested by the doctor as he has no other way to go about it. It is a very specialized profession and only someone who has been trained in this profession can do the treatment. Now definitely a candidate who got admission into a medical college because of reservation and then again a job in a government hospital cannot be as competent as another candidate who has entered the profession solely on the basis of his merit. Think about the loss in totality that the society and the country is suffering because of the reservation system whereby someone who is more deserving to enter this profession is being left out and someone who is much less deserving gets an opportunity to study and then again gets priority when entering the professional career also. Will the person who got admission into a medical college because there was seats reserved for him be as good and competent as another one who was much better and deserving.

There is no doubt that this will hold true for all professions be it engineers, doctors management graduates, teachers or any other profession. The system of reservation not only denies opportunity to more deserving candidates but also lowers the quality of the total workforce of the society which in turn affects the efficiency and the output that society gets finally from its productive workforce as a whole.

I am sure after more than 60 years of independence it is time to review the whole thing regarding reservation and find a better way to bring up the people who are in the lower section of the society. The sad part is that instead of looking at the whole thing of reservation in a constructive way, our politicians have used the noble thought of our earlier leaders to bring division among the people of the country and use different sections of people in the society as vote bank to win elections, playing with their sentiments based on caste, creed and religion. The percentage of reservation which was approx 22% at the time of independence has been increased to 50% in many states by bringing in other sections of the society under reservation. It is not that these politicians are genuinely concerned about the well being of these people. In fact it is the best and easiest way to divide the society and ensure pockets of votes by misguiding the people and playing on their emotions. The British people used to rule our country by using the policy of divide and rule and our politicians (definitely with a few exceptions) have been using this to further their own career and betterment by dividing the society on the basis of caste, creed and whatever other division they can think of so that they can come to power and exploit the people instead of genuinely working for the betterment of the society in general and the country as a whole.

Let me take the case of two of the biggest states in the country in terms of population UP and Bihar whose people or electorate send the max no of MPs to the Lok Sabha. These two states have one the highest poverty and some of the most backward areas in the country. When I used to study in Kanpur during 1986-90, at least I had not seen load shedding and shortage of electricity, but today after 23 years instead of improvement the condition has gone from bad to worse. The overall security situation has also worsened. If you look at the leaders who have come to power during this period you will find that in most of the cases the party or leader has been voted by the electorate on the basis of religion or caste. Same was the case with Bihar, where it is was even more easier to exploit the sentiment of the people as the percentage of poor and uneducated people is still more. Politicians have tried to secure votes by exploiting the sentiments of caste and religion. Political leaders go to their constituencies before election time, asking for votes and make promises which they do not have any intentions of fulfilling. In fact most of them cannot be seen in their constituency till it is time for the next elections. Politicians are voted by people to be their representatives but once elected these same politicians feel they have been sent to rule and use their term to secure their future and also their family members, making it a ticket to their future security. Unless there is inclusive development wherein all sections of the society is benefitted the country as a whole will not be able to able to progress and the true potential will never be realized. It is not that all politicians or bureaucrats are corrupt, but the whole system has become so polluted that honest and good people are not able to work. Honest officers are either being transferred or given insignificant positions when they try to work in a way which is against the wish of the politicians or the nexus between the politicians and mafia which maybe in mining, land, sand and anywhere where there is easy and corrupt money. The people having big stakes in mining, sand or real estate in extreme cases go to the extent of eliminating an honest official in case they are not able to bend them as per their requirement. There have been many cases where honest police and public administration officials had to pay with their lives for trying to do their duty in an honest way, and not doing as per the wish of the rich and powerful.

It is this exploitation whereby rich becomes richer and poor becomes poorer that leads people to revolt. It is this exploitation and divide between rich and poor that gives rise to movements like Maoism and make the exploited easy prey for terrorist groups and underground organizations. If we look carefully we will find that terrorism problem takes birth in mostly backward regions or countries. When people see that there is discrimination and exploitation whereby they do not see any improvement under the current scenario and circumstance they are forced to fight back and become easy prey for someone like a Osama Bin Laden.

As mentioned earlier it could be the case with under developed regions like in Bihar, MP, Orissa, Andhra or even in many cases among the backward section of the affluent countries whereby a certain section of the population feels that they have been exploited or have been treated in an unjust way. As the saying goes when you are pushed to the wall and there is no way of going back then only way is to fight back.

Not only this corruption and exploitation is depriving the more deserving people from being in the right place enabling them to make meaningful contribution towards the society and forcing people into the hands of terrorist and underground groups but in fact it is endangering the whole fabric of the society and affecting every aspect of existence and survival of human race in the planet. A good and recent example is the devastating floods in Uttarakhand, which could have been avoided to a great extent if the environment would not have been so brazenly played with by cutting trees and making human establishments. The utter disregard for protecting our trees, forests, rivers and other natural resources for short term monetary gain of few people will definitely make these kind of disasters more common in the years to come.

A PROGRESSIVE WAY OF THINKING

With the changing world where information is readily available and people are connected to each other through mass media and information technology leaders and society should start looking at things with a changed perspective.

I would like to mention here that good things are also happening and in many cases things are changing. In our country there are organizations who take kids from the street and give them education. But it has been found that the drop our ratio of these kids from the schools are very high. Maybe their span of attention is very low, they are not able to appreciate what is being taught to them or they feel claustrophobic sitting in a regular classroom which is very normal for a kid who is not used to this system of education from the childhood. One way of looking at could be that maybe vocational education would be more useful and effective for these type of kids, something which is more practical and interesting than regular, monologue in a typical classroom. This kind of study and training which is less bookish and more practical could be more interesting for these kids and they could see an immediate future once they get this kind of training from the point of view of earning a livelihood. Even their parents would be more interested in this kind of education as in many cases the kids are not only their child but hands to support the family. It will also be better utilization of resources with tangible outcome in terms of showing the kids a way to earn a respectable earning and progress in their life.

For the society to progress and the country to have its rightful place as one of the major players in world economy it is of outmost importance that there should be free flow of ideas, investment and importance should be given to research and development, money and efforts should be put into development of infrastructure, there should be efforts to reduce outdated rules and regulation and also remove bureaucratic hurdles. It should be clear that the job of government and politicians is to make policies and laws that will facilitate the development of industry and not run industries. Often it is culture and not politics that determines the success of the society but politics can change the culture by playing a positive and forward thinking role. This could be the way politicians should look at their roles to bring about positive change in the society. After years of keeping themselves disconnected from the world and following strict communism, China leaders decided to change and embraced foreign brands and expertise whereby they made it very easy for high end industries to invest in China and help develop the industrial base. The leaders in China realized after years of closed door policy and protectionism that best solution to overcome rural poverty is focus on development which will generate employment opportunities.

With the development of industry, it was normal that people were drawn off land into industry and out of farms into cities bringing out a huge portion of society from poverty. It helped in both ways, lot of people got absorbed into new industries and income from farming was distributed among much lesser no of people. China has been able to maintain a growth rate of 8-10 % for almost two decades bringing a vast population out of poverty. Policies which are not market friendly will not only hinder the flow of foreign investment and technology, but will also slow the growth of local industry thereby slowing down the entire process of development and progress of society.

The future is in research and upgrading of technology. It is not in BPO which can be done by any country with a sizcable population of English speaking population as has been demonstrated by a small country like Phillipines overtaking India in terms of BPO business. The future is in cutting edge technology which needs expertise like development of high end software, 3D printing, Nano technology which involves control of matter at atom or molecule stage, Bio technology. This would involve a lot of investment in terms of education, research and free flow of ideas and allowing and creating an environment whereby foreign companies will feel enticed and secure to invest in our country. It has to be noted here that only research and investment will not be enough as for progress ultimately it is very important to turn abstract ideas and theory into practical, useful and market acceptable tangible products. Any new product has a U shaped curve whereby at the top is idea leading to research and high level industrial design. Then comes detailed engineering plan. At the bottom of U is the actual manufacturing. At the top end again on the other side is marketing, sales and after sales servicing. The money is to be made at the top of U and there is least margin to be had in manufacturing. America is very good at the activities at the top of the curve which has enabled it to be the top economic power for decades and surely will hold the position in years to come. In Indian and Asian schools students are good at memorizing, taking tests and scoring good marks in examination but there is very little focus and encouragement on the aspect to developing the thinking process. In most cases the interaction between teachers and students is monologue whereby teachers teach and students learn what is being taught. In America there is engagement between the teachers and students and their culture encourages problem solving, questioning authority and thinking practically. It also allows people to fail and give them second chance so that they can try again if someone has the faith in his ability thereby encouraging innovation. It can be seen that American companies has the maximum no of patents and also highest no of Nobel prize winners in technology sector. There are many examples to show that again America is very good at marketing and sales. They have been able to build iconic brands like Coke and Mac Donalds, Pepsi, Starbucks, which does not need any rocket science but the capability to present the whole package in a way which is liked and craved for by people in any part of the world making them not only multinational but global brands.

Here I would like to mention that in terms of thinking differently in a new way found the observation made by Mr Taleb in his book Black Swan very interesting. He mentions that only stability is instability and uncertainty is the only certainty. He argues that we can never predict the next big thing that will change our lives like a terrorist attack, earthquake or a tsunami. So best way to prepare ourselves is to accept it and prepare to respond to any situation that comes. The British Empire started deteriorating when instead of medicine and engineering the elite became more interested in studying Roman history, literature which did not help in development or led to progress. The idea is to be resilient, prepare to bounce back from the disruption or a disaster. He presents that this could be the way to demoralize the terrorists as if they feel people are not terrorized their whole purpose is defeated. Found this line of thinking very interesting and different. I think it is the ability to think in a different way that will go a long way in not only improving the lives of the people but also help a nation to progress and solve a lot of problems which we find in the society.

In the changing environment and scenario our educational institutions should think and look at ways to say teaching economics or political science whereby students are encouraged to look at things with a new perspective or angle. After the end of cold war and America becoming the lone superpower it seems the think tank there believes that any problem in any part of the world has a military solution. An example could be they created AFRICOM with their commander and staff to ensure solving African problem. But for people there this is another kind of imperialism. In the changing scenario it would be much more fruitful to look at the process of engagement than unilateral action. It could be that America is the lone super power today but trying to find a military solution to problems in today scenario is not very wise and result oriented. For every nation it is imperative to think in a different way and explore how to tackle different scenarios so that it is amicable and long lasting. It is not only in the case of America, but for any country in any region when dealing with smaller or economically or militarily weaker country. If the bigger country has a dominating policy there will be resentment and bad feeling while positive engagement will bring a feeling of camaraderie and friendly environment. Also in today's world any country to be the leader will have to accept that double standard will not be acceptable.

Recently USA made allegations against Sri Lanka that army shelling killed hundreds of families during the final days of the ethnic war with the Tamil tigers. But when drone attacks by US military kills hundreds of innocent people then they say it was collateral damage. The US attacked Iraq saying that Saddam Hussein has weapons of mass destruction. After the war ended no such weapon was found, in fact the people at the top just wanted an excuse to enable them to get rid of Saddam. They removed Saddam, their soldiers fought a war which they could never win totally and have now left the country leaving behind a divided country where the so called local government which came to power with the blessings of America have control over very small portion of the total area, a large portion being controlled by ISIS and the life of the people is much more miserable than what was before America invaded the country. Before America invaded the country majority of the people had a stability and security. Now we see a country in turmoil with violence increasing every day after the departure of the American troops. In fact it has become a place where Al Qaida has found a good foothold and presence is increasing by the day. In fact it has become a much more dangerous place than when Saddam was there. No country has the right to destroy another country like this. The situation is not very rosy in Afghanistan, though here the invasion at least had the right reason or logic. But the way of engagement was maybe not appropriate as Taliban is slowly gaining ground in many parts of the country and it could be that once the US forces are withdraw from the country, Taliban could very well be back at the helm. If that is the case what has been the use of the war and so much money being spent along with death of thousands of innocent people which is collateral damage if the Taliban is back after the US troops are withdrawn. Definitely it shows the failure of the basic thinking that every problem has a military solution. Yes military engagement maybe necessary in many cases but unless the problem is understood in totality and combined with engagement in most cases it will be seen that in long term the desired result is never achieved. How can a country say that they believe in the democratic process and impartial supporter of democracy when someone like Robert Gates the former defense secretary alleges that top US diplomat Richard Hollbrooke supported Hamid Karzai's rivals in the hope of pushing the polls to a second round so that Mr Karzai would loose. Mr Gates is further quoted writing "It was ugly, our partner the President was tainted and our hands were dirty as well. Again revelations by US whistleblower Mr Snowden shows that NSA used to overhear and record telephonic conversation of top world leaders including that of German Chancellor Ms Angela Merkel whom they call one of their very important ally. On the other hand let us take the case of Indian consular official Devyani Khobragade which has led to the deterioration of relations between US and India. Whether she is wrong or faked the visa of her domestic help is a point to be debated and argued. But for sure the way she was handcuffed and strip searched is not acceptable in today's scenario. US argued that diplomatic immunity is not extended to consular officials and as such the case against Ms Devyani cannot be dropped. It was very clear that America has double standards, one for its own people and another for people coming from other countries. It becomes more complicated when one takes the case of the American been held in Pakistan for gunning down two people. US used all the pressure and forced to release him claiming diplomatic immunity though he was not a diplomat and in fact a contract worker working for Blackwater which was providing contract service to American intelligence agency. To be able to be seen truly as world leader only military and technological superiority is not enough but it is more important to be able to be fair and also walk the talk and most importantly should follow the path of engagement instead of suspicion and warfare. US is in the enviable position of being the military leader after the disintegration of the USSR, but to be the world leader in true sense it should be able to change its policy of domination to a policy of engagement in true sense and it should also change the thinking that any problem in any part of the world has a military solution to it. Very recently Mr Obama in one of his speeches mentioned that US has to change its image of being on permanent war footing to be more safer. It is a great and very courageous comment to make by the President. But in reality unless the various agencies like CIA and NSA which play a major role in shaping the policies of America bring about a change in way things are being looked at, it will be very difficult for even Mr Obama to bring any actual change at the ground level.

Not only in military terms but also in terms of financial matters it seems the leader of the world thinks not about engagement but follow a policy of what suits it best. Of course it is but natural to think about what is best for your country. But in case of America, who is both the financial and military super power and as a leader to have its rightful place they have to think a little differently. It is high time that America not only thinks about itself but starts thinking about how its policies and actions affects the globe in the long run. Say today America may feel that they are right in supporting or promoting a group or sect in the Middle East world just because that group is opposed to the current regime in Iran, though this particular group is spreading hatred and sectarianism. But instead of having such a short sighted view they should look at past history and towards the overall peace and well being and thereby instead of giving their support to this group, try their best to stop their activities with all their resources available as any organization or group which tries to divide people by talking of hatred or sectarianism cannot be good for anyone and could one day turn out to be another Frankenstein. Also it should be clear that such a group will be of no use in overthrowing the regime in Iran, except for being a nuisance that is causing division by exploiting the sentiments of the people and in fact will one day start spreading hatred for America and western world also, as the leaders of these groups have to find some issue which keeps them relevant and allows them to hold their influence over a certain percentage of population so that their sources of funding do not dry up and they can carry on with their subversive and divisive activities. In today's world where action or events in one place has an impact on many other places as things are so interconnected, countries like US, EU, China has to consider what effect its policy will have on others and world as a whole. Commenting on the weakening of the currencies in the developing and emerging markets like Turkey, Russia, India to some extent due to US cutting on Federal Stimulus in an interview Mr Raghuram Rajan, the RBI Governor very rightly pointed out that countries should take into account the effect of their policies on the other countries. US will definitely not reverse its policy on Federal Stimulus and slowly increasing the interest rates till it feels that it is not hampering its economic recovery, no matter what affect it has on the big economies like Brazil, Turkey, Russia or India apart from other emerging economies., On the other hand when it comes to China, the US has been on a long battle with the

Chinese leaders to make its currency more stronger and at a much faster pace to enable American products to be more competitive. They want Indian policy makers to open up the economy more and to new sectors like Insurance, retail and other sectors which could open up business for American businesses.

Let us take another case of the Middle East where Israel gets total support of US in almost everything. In 1982 Ariel Sharon invaded Lebanon with the idea of destroying the PLO and making Lebanon a satellite state. Israel with its military might and backing of US was able to defeat the combined Arab nation forces of Egypt, Syria and Jordan. At the end of six day war Israel was able to take Gaza Strip & Sinai Peninsula from Egypt, West Bank from Jordan and Golan Heights from Syria. But even after this military might was it able to destroy the PLO. It was a momentary win as the PLO recovered back with time but as a aftermath of the Lebanon invasion it led to the growth of another militant organization called Hezbollah which is a well organized force and a constant source of trouble for Israel. These show that military might may give a short term victory but for a long term solution there has to be engagement and richer and powerful nations have to demonstrate that they are not exploiting, the smaller or the weaker parties.

Similarly there is need to look at leadership from a new point of view in every place whether it is small or big organizations. Let us take the case of family which is the smallest unit in the society. In earlier days in our country people used to mostly stay in joint families where the decisions taken by the eldest male member was binding and accepted by all in the family without any questioning. With the changing lifestyle and independence first the joint family concept went and now even in nuclear families where both wife and husbands are working either by choice or the necessity to supplement the income, if the husband tries to dominate and tries to impose his decisions all the time it is not acceptable and in extreme cases results in separation. Same is the case in any organization where there are hundreds of people working together. No longer a leader can expect to get respect and good results from his team and sub ordinates if he tries to run a company in a dominating way. The way to go in the changing environment is by engagement where you try to take the opinion of your team and take the right decisions based on due deliberation taking into account the viewpoint of the team members and explaining why it would be best to choose a particular course of action. Also a leader has to be flexible and should have the ability to adapt to the changing environment and situation. It is often seen that a person who was very successful in one company is not able to perform to the desired expectations in another company. It is often seen that the same person whose style of working in a particular company was very much in line with that particular environment as well as internal and external factors involved is not suitable to another organization where the culture is different and the working requirements are different.

The sooner any leader is able to analyze the factors and adapt himself as per the requirements of the new organization the better his chances of success.

It is not only the leaders but all the employees working in an organization who have a very important role to play as it is not the leaders only who can shape the present and future of an organization but it is the whole team. Team work is essential in every field, be it sports, family, army, company, or whatever organization it maybe. Let us take the case of a cricket team, it could have the best leader but if it has a weakness in any department like batting, bowling or even fielding it cannot be world beater. The entire team has not only to be good in all departments but should be able to adapt and perform in different situations and conditions to be able to be the best team. A very good example is the West Indies team of the 80s who could perform anywhere in the world with their team. I have worked in quite a few organizations and have found that in almost all cases sub ordinates are equally responsible in making leaders into thinking that boss is always right. People feel that if they do not agree to what boss says they will not get promotions or they may loose their job, so instead of saying what is good for the organization they will say what the boss wants to hear. The main idea is to please the boss instead of doing what is good for the company. In rare cases it could be that one is treated badly for differing with the ideas or opinion of boss but mostly from my experience I have seen that if you are correct and able to make your point in a logical way without hurting the sentiment or showing disrespect boss usually takes your point of view in the right spirit and in fact appreciates for giving your opinion and helping to arrive at a better decision.

As per a survey done in UK one third of the employees said that trust between them and senior management as weak. Another study by Forum Corp a Boston based consultancy firm found in their survey that one third of the workers nowadays trust business leaders less than in the past. In fact more surprisingly 43% of managers said employees trust bosses less now as compared to the past years. So definitely there is something wrong here either in way bosses or management operate or in the perception of the people. Either way the organization suffers as dissatisfaction and lack of trust are two things which greatly affects the environment and the performance of the people. On one hand due to distrust subconsciously or knowingly employees give less than 100% in their work as they will have the feeling that no matter how well they perform their boss will not judge it fairly and they feel it is good enough that they only put in so much effort and work so that their bosses cannot point a finger at them and their job is not at risk. These employees will never go the extra yard which could make a big difference to the bottom line of the company. Lack of trust is also equally detrimental to any organization as then people are more concerned about protecting their asses and spend more time to ensure how they cover themselves when there is a problem or a review. These people also try to find ways how to pass on the blame in case something goes wrong or something comes up which is not as per the expectation of the boss. When there is an environment of distrust and fear in the organization it will be seen that a big portion of the time of the employees goes in trying to plot against fellow colleagues and thinking about how to protect oneself in the event of any failure and ultimately the company is the sufferer as this time would else have been used for productive purpose. It is very important to build an environment of trust and team work among the employees for any organization to be a good organization where the people will go the extra yard to do things which can not only add to the bottom line but can be crucial to the survival of a company in today's environment of cut throat competition. The bosses should be very much aware that as they do, the employees and sub ordinates are also monitoring the bosses and seniors. Bosses must realize that they can make mistake and if they do they should be able to accept it and say sorry. This will go a long way to build trust and people will start respecting him. If they find that boss takes credit for a job well done by a sub ordinate he will never get respect from the people under him. I was very lucky to get a boss in the early part of career from whom I could learn how to gain the trust and respect of sub ordinates. While working in Mafatlal I was lucky to get a boss who without saying directly showed by his actions that if a subordinate does well than he should be getting the credit but for some reason if the sub ordinate makes a mistake the boss should have the courage to face the top management and take the blame on him or at least try to share the responsibility. This not only develops a very healthy working relationship but also encourages the person to go out of his way to work and make things happen. I would like to give here an example to illustrate this in a better way.

After my first trip to South America, when I returned to office and went to my superior and told about the new orders that I booked he immediately took me to the head of marketing and told him about the same and in fact that was the second time I was meeting the head of marketing after my joining the company. He gave the whole credit to me without mentioning that some of the orders that I had booked was a result of an earlier trip that he had made to the same market just 3 months back and some of the contacts were in fact developed by him in that trip. In another case I made a mistake of selling a wrong quality in terms of weight of fabric that was committed to the customer. When the shipment sample was received by the customer and he found that weight of actual fabric was less than what was committed to him he refused to take the goods. I went to my boss and told him the whole thing. He went with me to our superior and said that there was some problem with quality of goods and that maybe we would have to give some discount to solve the matter. Finally we were able to settle the issue by giving a discount of 10 percent. I had learnt a very good lesson and never made this mistake later on during my career and later on always used to check with technical people before committing anything to the customer. These two incidents not only gave me a lot of confidence but also respect for my boss. I have tried to follow what I learnt from him in all the different organizations I have worked in and found how useful it is as I have myself moved up in the ladder.

There is another very interesting incident which had occurred when I was working in another company. We were trying to develop business with Marks and Spencer. They wanted a particular sample and said that if everything goes right they would like to place some initial quantities with us. I gave instructions to production in charge to prepare the sample and the sample was sent. After a few days fax comes directly to the Managing Director saying the sample had failed. I was immediately called by my superior when I was inside the factory and was told that Managing Director was very upset about this and he wanted to call a meeting to find what had happened. In fact he told me to find who made the mistake and be ready with an explanation. We have a finish in textiles which is termed as easy to iron meaning a certain chemical is applied so that cotton shirts can be ironed easily after washing and it does not crease so much on wearing. The customer wanted this finish with mild peaching which is like brushing to give a smoother feel to the fabric. Since I was in factory I went to production head and discussed the thing with him. Then we realized that to expedite things we had done peaching on ready fabric due to which the bonding between the chemical and cotton was broken. I immediately took an appointment with the Managing Director and explained him the whole thing. He just told me to send another sample at the earliest with a note explaining to the customer why the first sample had failed. The production head was very happy as he did not have to face the Managing Director and also the valuable time of many top executives was not wasted. From then on the production head used to go out of his way to help me. Also his sub ordinates used to help me a lot and always used to handle my orders with special care so that there were no delays. Ultimately it helped the company also as there was an environment of trust and co operation between production and the marketing teams.

Let us take the case of recent success of AAP (Aam Admi party) in Delhi state elections. It is a party formed just a year back with the promise to work for removal of corruption from the political system. Whether they are successful or how much they are able to deliver on the promises only time will tell. But the important point to consider here is that people want change. People in general are fed up with the current political scenario and have lost faith on the mainline political parties to deliver and so ready to try someone who does not have any political or governing experience. They are fed up with leaders promising the moon at the time of election and not delivering when comes to power. The common people is frustrated with the endemic corruption in every sphere of life and wants to bring a change to the culture of corruption and bribery and kickbacks. The important thing to note here is that people do not want change just for the sake of change. Leaders who have performed in the perception of the majority of population are being re-elected and in coming days it would be performance and ability to deliver when in power that will keep leaders in power rather than promises and playing on factors like caste and religion. The people in general and youngsters in particular want change and want to be a part of a new beginning.

AAP was able to come as a political entity due to the vacuum that has been created due to populist politics being practiced by the mainstream parties. When the AAP was formed all political parties said that it will fail as a political party. Then when they decided to contest the Delhi election both Congress and BJP leaders were not even ready to consider them as opponents saying that they will not get any seats. Now they are saying they are a Delhi based party and can have no impact in National elections.

The rise of AAP is not only because of their USP of clean politics and inclusive governance but has been equally aided by the failure of mainstream political parties and their self denial that people are fed up with populist politics that they practice and the endemic corruption in every sphere of life in the country. If we see any mass poll that have been conducted in the country it will be seen that politicians, bureaucrats, and police will come at the bottom of popularity list and top in the list of corruption.

It is this vacuum and resentment among people which have allowed AAP to make such an impact in such a short time of their entering politics. Now we see that at least its success has made the leaders in Congress and BJP to rethink their strategy for the upcoming elections and hopefully they will change for the positive.

I was very much happy to hear an incident narrated by one of my colleagues from Bangladesh. He had been on a trip to UK and was in the restaurant for dinner. He met a girl who was working there and on enquiring came to know that the girl was from India. She was studying there and to meet part of her expenses used to work in that place on part time basis. While talking to her my colleague enquired about her future plans and where she would like to work after completion of her studies. She told him that she was there so that she could get a better education but as regards working she just said Mera Bharat Mahan. This is a big change from a few years back when people who used to go to study abroad only used to think of working outside due to both monetary factor and also job satisfaction. With change in the job opportunities and better facilities many people are coming back to work in their own country. It is very encouraging to see Indians wanting to come back to contribute to the country. Many of the Indians who came back leaving their secure jobs and all the facilities they have abroad say that they find that they are doing here something more exciting and self fulfilling. In many cases small efforts and changes here can make big difference in the outcome, which is difficult to notice in a developed economy.

There is a need to educate and relook at how we utilize our resources and protect our environment. We take the air that we breathe, the water that we use for drinking and other purposes for granted. Unless we are all aware and start respecting the nature and our environment we are headed for disaster if not today then in the future. Thinks can change pretty drastically and things we take for granted may not be so in very quick time. Recently all schools, restaurants and offices had to be closed in Charleston, Virginia due to contamination of the river water from leakage in a chemical factory.

We see a lot of time that cities in China like Beijing has smog cover most of time and stories of schools being closed as it could be too dangerous for kids. Before the Olympics in Beijing a lot of factories were closed to reduce the pollution to manageable levels for athletes to perform during the premier sports event. Awareness about protection of our environment should be inculcated among the kids from the time they go to schools. There are lessons in social studies in schools which have chapters regarding environment and what damages it may cause if we pollute our environment. But the kids in schools just study it, memorize it for writing at the time of examination and forget about it once the exam is over. It could be simple things like asking the students how much water they used for the day. Did they see that any tap was kept open by the maid or any member of the family and if so did they take the trouble of closing it down. There could be documentaries or visuals to show the kids where they can see how people suffer if they do not get clean water and air so that it makes a lasting impression on the young minds leading to actual learning and awareness instead of studying only for academic purpose. I have seen in many houses that since parents can afford to pay the bills they do not bother to put off the lights, fans or air conditioners. They are not only wasting the valuable resources impacting the environment, depriving others who could have used this wasted electricity but also giving a wrong education to their child who will feel that it is very natural to use resources as he wishes if they can afford it. If we do not look into protection of the environment our future generation is definitely going to suffer and curse us. I read and hear about global warming due to pollution and emission of poisonous gases into the environment, depletion of the ozone layer, thinning of the ice layer in the poles. These are very technical things and I cannot comment much on these issues as there are experts who are studying these things and observing the things. But definitely can see that cutting of trees and clearing of forests is changing the environment as places like Bangalore which used to have very moderate temperature throughout the year are reaching temperature like 36-37 degree during the summer, many wild animals in different part of the world are becoming endangered species and their population is reducing gradually. It is inevitable that with increasing population and development taking place in every part of the world there will be changes, land will be cleared up for cultivation, factories will come up, there will be more vehicles on the road, more use of natural resources. But it is the duty of every individual and the government in particular to ensure that things are done in a planned way and what can be avoided should be avoided. How can any government allow tanneries and textile factories to dump the toxic wastes into waters and river bodies polluting the very water which is the lifeline of existence in this universe. Just if the government is serious and strict about not allowing any factory which do not have proper treatment of waste water and disposal to operate it can stop to a large extent the the pollution of the water bodies by these toxic chemicals. If the officials and the ministers would have had the learning from childhood about the importance of protecting the environment they would have thought many a times before making money by allowing factories to run without proper treatment and disposal of water. There are many tanneries and factories which use a lot of water every day and dump this toxic water directly into streams and rivers especially in the developing countries like India, Bangladesh, etc. These are been reported and local officials and environment departments working for the government are aware of the things but these factories are being allowed to operate year after year. I do not suggest that someone wakes up one fine morning and gives the decision to close down all the factories, as this will lead to another problem of loss of job for huge number of people. A better and more practical solution to tackle will be not to allow any factory to start the operation unless it has a proper mechanism of treatment and disposal of harmful material and in case of factories which are in operation they should be given a practical time frame within which to put in place system for proper treatment and disposal. In fact no private company will dare to start a factory without ensuring that they have put in place proper treatment and disposal mechanism if they know they will not be able to get through by bribing and using influence of political leaders and government officials. In fact government should have designated industrial zones which could be given for development and people will be able to set up industries only in those industrial zones. There it is much easier to monitor the factories and also common facilities can be built for treatment of water as per the requirement of various industry type. It will also solve the problem of unplanned growth of industries, encroaching of farm lands for making factories and also cutting and clearing of forests to set up business establishments.

Another very important thing is inclusive development, whereby all sections of the society is benefitted, In today's world and in years to come inequality is becoming a very big issue. It is one of the reasons of dissatisfaction and division among people. politicians, bureaucrats, economists, social think tanks and the elite class in society have to all think how to arrive at a mcchanism so that we can have an inclusive development rather than rich getting richer and poor languishing behind in their same sorry state. I think everyone will remember the slogan of India shinning during the last election held in 2004. In fact the BJP was so confident of winning the elections on the basis of development and progress done by the country that they brought the national elections forward by a few months to en cash on the vibrancy of the economy. But to their utter surprise and the predictions they were not elected as the development was visible in the urban areas and people in rural areas had not seen India Shinning. This is not to take away the good work and development done during the Vajpayee government but the development was not inclusive, the poorer sections and the rural areas had not felt the effects of the developments which was much more apparent in the urban areas.

Here would like to share a very nice story that I read. An Anthropologist proposed one game to the kids of African Tribal people. He placed a basket of fruits near a tree and made them stand 100 meters away. Then he announced that whoever reaches there first will get all the fruits in the basket. After explaining he started the race by saying ready steady and go. The kids all caught each other's hands and ran towards the tree together, divided the fruits among them and enjoyed it.

The Anthropologist was surprised with the action of the kids and asked them the reason for doing so. The kids explained that how one kid can be happy when all the others are sad. I AM BECAUSE WE ARE. It shows what it means to share and be happy all together. A very simple story but with a very meaningful morale.

Now it is easy to say we have to have inclusive development, but in practical purpose it is difficult to achieve. Many books and articles have been written about the failure of Communism. It is true that Communism failed, but I would not say the free market economy as is been practiced now is a success too as it has failed to address the issue of inclusive development. The Government has to work sincerely in a country like India and most countries in the world to find ways to uplift the total population. This can only be done by creating opportunities. If you give food to somebody today, he will come back again the next day when the food is finished. People should have a chance to succeed, which will give them hope for the future. Of course in many cases it has to be backed by basic nutrition, access to education and scholarships. There is a need to relook at how best to utilize the resources that we have including the large youth and employable population. It has been seen in general that while development a country goes through three basic sectors, first is the agriculture, then manufacturing and then into service sector. If we see the distribution as per 2012 data, agriculture constitutes 17.4 percent, manufacturing 25.8 percent and service sector 56.9 percent of India's GDP. In comparison, for China it is 10.1 percent is agriculture, 45.3 percent is manufacturing and 44.6 percent is service sector. It can be seen that as an economy progresses percentage of agriculture slowly reduces and manufacturing increases and then majority contribution comes from the service sector. But in case of India service sector has over taken, manufacturing quite some time back. It means without full development and reaching the potential for manufacturing sector, service sector has grown to be more than 50 percent of the GDP. Yes India is a leading player in Information technology in the world, but we see service sector cannot generate as many jobs as the manufacturing sectors. There is a big potential for the development of the manufacturing sector which has lagged behind due to many factors, like the feasibility of getting suitable land, long bureaucratic process to get the clearance and license, availability of clear cut guidelines for availability of raw materials, politicians stopping projects for the sake of populist politics, lack of infrastructure and power, political instability and security concerns and to some extent availability of skilled manpower. Even in a highly developed economy like Germany, manufacturing still constitutes 28.1 percent of the GDP. This along with the work ethics and quality makes Germany the leading economy in Europe with very less unemployment even during the years of global financial crisis. Even in a country like Switzerland which is mainly famous for its banking and chocolates, manufacturing still comprises more than 27 percent of the total GDP. China realized that to employ the vast population who will be moving out of agriculture with the development of economy, they have to have a very vibrant and expanding manufacturing sector as it can employ the biggest number of people and to facilitate the same equal importance was given to the development of infrastructure like roads, ports, etc. Though China has been practicing Communism politically its leaders realized long back that for the economy to prosper and to generate employment for its huge population it has to move out of the communist policy, when it comes to business and the economy. The Government in our country has to find ways to develop infrastructure and facilitate the development of manufacturing sector if the economy is to be vibrant and to generate employment for larger portion of the population. Unless we can strengthen our infrastructure and the manufacturing sector we will never be able to reach the full potential and will be a promise which could have been. There are many cases to see what difficulties industry face in our country, like the case of Tata's who had to abandon their project for manufacturing Nano cars in West Bengal. After going far ahead with their plant due to opposition from then opposition party Trinamool Congress. JSW 35,000 crore rupees steel project in West Bengal has been shelved due to long delays for red tape and also no clear policy regarding the availability of raw material to come from Orissa. There will be many projects which have been conceived but could not go much further beyond the project stage due to the various difficulties faced by industry in the country as mentioned earlier.

Instead of improving infrastructure and creating a conducive environment for the development of industry the Govt and the politicians take the easy route of populist measures like saying that they are not allowing foreign investments to protect the local industry. In fact they are doing more harm by this as they are then reducing the choice available to the people, and allowing inferior goods to be in the market and available to people. In many cases these inferior products are the inputs for the next product leading to lowering of the quality of the subsequent product also.

During the last five years India has had a low growth rate of 5-6 percent which is too low for the country. It has been said that the country needs at least 8-9 percent growth to bring the huge population below poverty line into the main stream. Looking at today's political climate it may not be possible for either of the two national parties to form a government on their own and they may have to run the country with the aide of other parties. So there needs to a basic change of mindset among the politicians that they cannot play with the basic interest of the country for their petty needs. Unless the economy is restored back to the high growth path and the engines of growth are kick started, the whole economy in general and business in particular will flounder and instead of adding jobs, there will be loss of jobs. We have seen that one of the best strategy of the ruling party is to dole out free sops and make commitments for newer one if voted into power. They are just thinking about how to come to power for the next 5 years knowing fully well that this is not sustainable in the long run and secondly the saddest part is in most cases it does not reach people who are supposed to be benefitted as most of it is gobbled by politicians and the government machinery.

Any government that runs the country has to think about developing proper infrastructure for growth in medium and long term which will be sustainable. We have seen that Indians are very much innovative and resilient due to which despite poor infrastructure and red tape business is developing, so one can imagine what potential there is if they get the support of government in terms of infrastructure and clear policy guidelines, with reduction in corruption. If red tape is reduced automatically there will be less possibility of bribery and corruption as the files and clearance points will be reduced. Government should pass legislations and bring reforms which will make getting clearances for projects easier and faster. They should also support industries and agriculture with incentives and subsidies where actually required not as populist measures but after proper study of the potential of an industry, actual requirement, analyzing what other countries are doing and what kind of employment generation is possible.

Government should promote and encourage the growth of small businesses as it has been seen that the SMEs have the potential to generate maximum employment opportunities. There should be well planned road map for development of business clusters whereby SMEs supply to bigger manufacturing companies so that the whole region and its neighbor hood comes up and there is employment generation. The government should make policies to this end and also offer incentives for the growth of such business clusters. It has been seen that though the SMEs are very vital cog in the wheel for maintaining growth and employment generation they do not get financial support from banks and financial institutions. Here government has a very important role to play so that the SMEs are able to get the required financial support

The big business houses who are flush with excess funds should also play a role by helping to develop smaller industries. They do not have to do charity but allocate funds to innovative and serious companies who have the potential to develop product and technologies related to their fields. This will not only help to develop business clusters around the big business houses but will benefit the bigger businesses as it will help develop reliable and long lasting relationship and partners for supply of parts and material and at the same time help in overall development and growth of the region by the way of employment generation and thereby promote an inclusive development.

India can take a cue from China where the government after careful study sets the priorities for which sectors of business should be developed. After it has been identified then all kind of resources like human resource, raw material availability, power, infrastructure and financial support in form of lower interest rates are given and dedicated for the proper implementation and development of the sectors. So the government has a very important role to play and it should act as partners with business. It should be involved as mentioned earlier in identification of key industries that can bring in growth and also generate employment opportunities. It can then facilitate the growth of the identified sectors by making policies conducive to the development of the sector by ensuring availability of the resources, infrastructure and financial means.

Another very important area which can impact the sustainable growth in long term is by strengthening the ties between the educational centers and the businesses. Rather than providing education which is for doing jobs the colleges and institutes should also be breeding grounds for budding entrepreneurs. The students should be provided training relevant to a particular industry which is of interest to him, should be given confidence, contacts and means to get started. Big businesses should have dedicated centers in the educational institutes where they will not only give financial assistance but also send their senior executives to interact with the students and guide them by giving live and relevant examples and also training as required. The big businesses should have a small percentage of budget allocated to the funding of budding entrepreneurs.

What could be the things that could propel the country into a sustainable high and consistent and inclusive growth. Let us try to look at the things that the government should focus on for improving the overall condition of the people. The two most vital things that needs immediate focus is education and health. I have dealt with the condition of the education earlier in the book. Government has to study carefully and decide what percentage of the budget should be allocated for the purpose of education to have a real impact. Not only this it has to ensure that the money is utilized properly and does not go into the pocket of privileged few. As discussed before in detail an educated population is the biggest asset of the country as they have the capacity to judge right from wrong, take proper decisions, guide their own children and also difficult to manipulate in the name of caste and religion. I feel realizing this thing only political parties wants to ensure that vast majority of the population remain illiterate so that they can keep on manipulating them on the lines of caste and religion. It is the duty of the both the central and state governments to ensure that basic school education is made available to all in the country and not just by having a building in the villages but by ensuring that proper teaching is imparted to the kids in these schools.

The second most important thing is health. Basic health and medical facilities should be available for all including the remote villages. I remember going to a tea estate near Jorhat in Assam during my summer holidays as my uncle used to work there as a doctor. It is one the biggest tea estates in Assam. There used to be a proper hospital with the basic amenities close to the house of my uncle. He used to go there every day and in emergency cases also at any time of the night. It was only in very rare cases that he had to recommend the sick to go to the city for treatment. The best thing was he was very much satisfied with what he was doing and worked in that place till his retirement. So when a private company could afford to have the basic health requirement of its employees taken care of, I do not see any reason why the government cannot do it with the huge resources at its disposal if it has the will and the well- being of the population in mind. Maybe they will have to make it compulsory for every doctor working in Govt Hospitals to give at least a few days of theirs to the hospitals in villages and remote places, give special incentives like better pay packet for doctors who spend certain minimum number of days in remote areas, or maybe doctors who spend more than certain number of days in a year in remote area or villages for say 3-5 years, they could be eligible for faster promotion. There could be other innovative ways to ensure that minimum health care is available even to people staying in villages and remote areas. All it needs is the desire and the will power to make things happen. I am not suggesting here that any one should be forced but motivated to give service also for the better health of whole nation. Take the case of Israel where it is compulsory for everyone including the female population to have military training. As soon as someone turns 18 he/she is drafted into the military for training and have to give a minimum period of time to the military depending on whether the person is male or female.

Also another thing that has to be looked at is availability of food. After so many years of independence food security for all has to be ensured. Malnutrition should be tackled and brought to an end. It is only a healthy and vibrant population which can contribute to the productivity and growth of the country. It is a great opportunity for the country that in a few years we are going to be the youngest country in the world in terms of its population age. Utilized in the right way it can be the biggest asset, else like all other possibilities this would pass as another potential or opportunity lost. For such a big population and that too a young one, food requirements will be huge. This will require that government facilitates proper irrigation facilities, availability of fertilizer, seeds of better quality higher productivity, along with use of technology. It has to be seen how we can reduce the dependence of farming on the monsoon quality as not only one bad monsoon forces the farmers to be engulfed in a cycle of huge debts, it also results in higher prices of food due to shortage. With growing population, availability of land for agriculture will be getting scarce so only way is to get higher yield so that from the same land we can get more food. There has to be initiatives to use technology and real time data to improve assessment and management of farm products so that they can be stored for longer periods and also can be transported much faster to the destinations in case of perishable goods. It has to be ensured that there is proper distribution of the food that is produced and not the case of wheat or rice rotting in warehouses on one hand and poor people not even getting one good meal in the day.

Along with these things if government takes sincere initiatives to tackle the rampant corruption in every sphere of the life it will go a long way in building a vibrant nation which can stand on its foot and hold its head high in the world. Corruption is the biggest bottleneck in the development of the country and everyone is fed up of it. It is because of this frustration and looking for alternative that AAP was voted in Delhi to form the government. It is another case that they could not utilize the mandate given to them and looking at the upcoming Lok sabha elections tried to use it to their advantage by resigning from government. But general feeling was in the short period of time they were in power, Delhi had seen corruption going down quite substantially. If there is a will there is always a way. Sad part is India is still searching for someone who is strong enough and has the will to fight this endemic problem which has permeated into every strata of the society. Everyone from a peon to the highest person in any Government office thinks that it is their birthright to ask for money to get a small thing done. Anyone who is ready to pay money and can afford it gets his work done and rest has to languish till they can arrange for the money demanded by the officials. There are cases where even to get their pensions after serving for their whole life people have to pay money to ensure that files are moved from one table to another. It has become a way of life in our country and hampering progress in every sphere of life. You are caught for drunk driving, you go free if you pay money to police or you have connection who can put in a word for you, you need to get admission again same story, you want your file cleared or loan passed again pay money. It is not that it is restricted to government offices, it is everywhere where there is scope to make underhand money in cash or in kind. You want to get orders from buying offices of foreign brands you have to take care of the person handling the business either in cash or kind. It would not be right for me to be specific here but I have seen and heard this from reliable sources who have faced it personally. Again you want to be a supplier for private companies, you have to take care of person who is in charge of decision making authority. I remember a case when I was in college and had to go home during vacation. Floods are yearly occurrence in Assam and that time all road and train connection were disrupted due to heavy floods and only way to go was to take a flight from Kolkata. I was trying to get a plane ticket for two days but due to heavy rush was not possible and was informed that I could get a ticket after 7 days. Being a student I did not have money to survive for so many days, so though I was scared I approached the airline personnel and offered him Rs 500 which was a big amount in those days. To my relief it was accepted and I got a ticket to fly that very day. Since those days corruption has increased manifold. Whenever we discuss this among ourselves I find most of the people resigned to the fate that this is part of life and it is easy to say but practically impossible to tackle this endemic problem of corruption. I am an optimistic and still believe that it will take one strong leader who has the will and the guts to tackle this problem. There are examples of one leader turning the country around in Malaysia, Singapore and South Korea to name a few who are close to us. To be practical it may not be eliminated totally but if it is reduced by considerable amount we will see a sea change how the country progresses, at least bridges or flyovers will not be made with substandard material, subsidies meant for the people will not into the pockets of officials who are in charge of disbursing it, infrastructure development will be there of proper quality, funds which are being allocated for the hungry and for development of the rural areas will be utilized in much better way. Just to give a small example a new flyover was made in the Ultadanga in Kolkata, but within three months one span of the flyover came down along with a loaded truck. The first statement that came out was that this flyover was made during the time of the previous government, so a committee has to be formed to find out the reason for the mishap and the person responsible for it. It has been more than an year now but that span of the flyover is still where it fell down and the flyover remains un useable. With the reduction in corruption we will see that there is a sea change how the efficiency improves in every sphere of life that affects us. There is corruption even in the developed countries and will be practically impossible to eliminate but even if it is reduced by 80 percent of what we are seeing at the moment, it will add substantially to the all round development of the country and well being of the people.

Another very important thing to be looked into is the policy of reservation. It was initially brought into our constitution so that the backward SC and ST people could be brought into the mainstream of the society by reserving certain percentage initially something of approx., 22 percent in colleges and government jobs. I am sure while making the provision, it was not thought that even after 67 years of independence we not only have reservations but in fact in some states it has gone up to as high as 50 percent. It is not that politicians who have ensured that reservations continue and in fact in many states increased it, due to their sincere wish of bringing these people out of poverty or uplifting the backward sections. The main idea is to create divisions and use a particular community and caste as their permanent vote bank at the time of elections as outlined earlier. If someone from say Yadav community comes he/ she make provision for reservation of Yadavs, someone else from another caste comes to power he then brings reservation for that community, now it has been seen that in one state they are fighting for reservation of Jats. The very purpose for which reservation provision was made in the constitution has been defeated and it has become a tool in the hands of the politicians to create vote banks. In most cases it will be seen it is the well to do people of these different castes and community who are getting the benefit of the reservation policy, actually who do not need it at all. I am not against reservation per say, but I am totally against reservation the way it is being practiced at the moment. There has to be a way by which the benefit of reservation goes to people who actually deserve it so that over a period of time there is inclusive development of the whole country. One of the way to ensure that this benefit reaches the maximum no of people is by making a policy so that only one member of the family will be eligible for reservation and others will fall under the normal category. In this way over a period of time maximum number of people will be covered. Also it will seen that it is the educated people in this category who knows about reservation and as such they are able to take benefit of this facility. So even for this reservation policy to have the mass benefit it has to be ensured that basic education is available to all so that they know about the existence of this policy and can utilize it. Basically the idea is to ensure that the benefit of this policy is being utilized by the maximum number of people and goes to the people who actually deserve it. I am sure that if something like this would have been implemented from the day of independence then a lot more families would have been benefited and there could have much more inclusive uplifting of the people falling in this category. The current policy has multiple drawbacks. One it is being utilized by mostly those who actually do not need it any more and like dynasty goes to members of family whose maybe third generation is now using it since independence. Also it is being used by politicians to create vote banks and diving the country along caste lines. Thirdly by increasing the percentage of reserved seats for different categories, it is depriving good talent from entering into colleges and government jobs bringing in mediocrity in terms of people who are serving the country. A much better way of uplifting the condition of the people who are still lagging behind and in actual need of reservation is by having them based on the economic status. Then it will actually benefit the people who need it and over a period of time will have the desired effect of bringing a lot more people into the mainstream of the society. Again there has to some restrictions like one member of a family will get this benefit in which case a much larger population as a whole will be able to benefit within a much shorter time span. The automatic good thing that will happen in this case is that the politicians will not be able to divide the society along caste lines and they will have to think about more positive ways to secure vote at the time of elections. It will make them work during their tenure if they want to come to power the next time. The politicians will realize that they cannot exploit the electorate on the basis of caste and religion so they will be judged on basis of their honesty and the work they have done during the period when they were voted to power to represent their constituency. Then we will see that the country get the benefit from real democracy and we as Indians will be able to hold our heads in front of the world as people who live in a vibrant democracy.

This part will not be complete without throwing some light on the issue of religious polarization that the political parties have done for vote catching beside diving the people on the caste lines. The 2014 elections have shown that political parties are ready to go down to any level and use any means to garner votes no matter it destroys the very fabric of the secular country. Every political party has tried to show they are the only one who can protect the interest of either minority or the majority. Congress party has been playing the religion and caste card since a long time and have always used the minority card as their vote bank. Now there are many other parties who have learned the tricks of divisive politics and Congress having to face real competition where it cannot claim to be the sole protector of minority community has been forced to go down to the level where Mrs Sonia Gandhi meet, the Imam of Jama Masjid for him to appeal to the Muslims to vote for Congress party during the elections. It is sad to see that instead of speaking about their achievements during 10 years when they were ruling the country they have to focus on vote catching in lines of division on the basis of caste and religion. This is just taking Congress as an example as they being the ruling party had the best chance to talk of their work and achievements whereas other would have to tell that what they could do if voted to power. The country is dire need of someone who can unite the different castes and religion so that it can benefit from the united efforts of all sections of the society.

LOOKING FORWARD

I am sure the people of this country are looking towards their leaders to work for the inclusive development of the country. Besides corruption which is the one single biggest talking point people would like to see that whoever is elected to form the government should focus on long term sustainable development so that in years to come country can grow at a rate where more and more people will come out of poverty and will have a vibrant young India holding its rightful place in the world stage.

One biggest area to be focused on is creating job opportunities. The leaders have to think how to create jobs for millions of young people who are coming into the productive working age group. As discussed earlier for this the government has to make legislations and laws which makes it easier for the entrepreneurs to get clearances for new projects and also for foreign investors to invest in the country. This is one single biggest hindrance due to which many projects are stalled or remain in the board room drawing boards. Instead of making laws which act as hindrance or obstacle, they should find ways to simplify the procedure to start and run a business whether it is a local investment or from abroad. The simplified rules and lesser clearance process will not only encourage the people to bring in new projects but also will increase the efficiency and result in higher growth as things will be moving at a much faster pace.

At the same time lesser the clearance steps and red tape automatically less will be the chances of government officials and bureaucrats to do corruption.

There are many areas where foreign companies are not coming either due to bureaucracy or due to red tape in the system and in many cases foreign companies are reluctant as majority holding is not allowed. The government needs to look at objectively which are sectors that are of strategic importance from the point of view of safety and security of the country and also where actually investment from foreign companies may actually harm the local economy and may affect the livelihood of the people, instead of looking it from the point of vote bank and narrow thinking. Not only this for FDI to come to our country we have to create an environment and have facilities so that the top executives who come to India to run these companies have the quality of life which if not exactly same as what they are used to in their country, they are at least up to acceptable standards, in terms of education for kids, safety and security of their family, and other things. Creating job opportunities is not only important from the point of view of growth of economy only, but will also help in reducing a lot of social problems and unrest which are actually happening due to lack of development resulting in lack of opportunities to earn a meaningful livelihood. I am sure no youngster will like to join any underground organization or become a terrorist if he sees that he has the opportunity to lead a proper life staying within the society. If we see we will find that insurgency or Maoism is most prevalent in area where there is least development and where the young generation does not have opportunity to earn a meaningful livelihood, whether is it the North East,

Jammu & Kashmir, or the backward areas in the states of Orissa, Madhya Pradesh, Jharkhand, and Andhra Pradesh.

The next biggest hindrance is infrastructure. For any country to grow on a sustainable level for a long period of time especially for a country, like India which is so big and diverse with states and regions with vastly different levels of development there has to be a good infrastructure. Government should work on developing roads which is so essential for transportation of goods from one place to another. It not only makes things easier and faster but helps to increase efficiency and loss of resources like gasoline, spares, tyres, etc. In general if we compare the roads in our country with developed countries or even with China, they are much inferior and heavily congested. If we go to the villages there are still 40 percent villages where they do not have all weather roads or in many cases roads are non- existent. Due to this the transportation of agriculture products becomes difficult or takes much longer time. Coupled with road condition and hardly any availability of storage facilities, leads to lot of farm products not being properly distributed or left to rot either in the villages or during the long transportation time from the villages. The country has seen some developments as compared to say 20 years back but still there are many regions where a lot has to be done.

For any industry whether it is agriculture, service sector or manufacturing, availability of power is the most essential thing as without it no industry can survive. Uninterrupted power supply without fluctuations of voltage and current is like the lifeline of any industry. Like humans need air to survive, industry needs power. In today's competitive world any manufacturing industry which is capital intensive and has huge fixed costs if the operations cannot be run continuously without stoppages for power, it will never be viable. To keep the operations stopped due to power failure or say to run it by other means like having backup diesel generators, means additional costs and at the same time loss of production, makes the operation sick.

It not only eats into the narrow margins on which most of industries have to survive but also causes additional damage in terms of delays especially affecting factories which are into exports. Availability of power has been one of the main reasons why we have seen so many projects coming up in the state of Gujarat and people been keen on investing there even if some other parts could be more viable in terms of lower labor costs and nearer to the source of raw materials. I have seen myself how the availability of power can impact the growth of industry during my 12 years of working in Bangladesh. Here most of the capital intensive industries mostly textiles run on own gas generators as the electricity from government is erratic and there is lot of fluctuation. It has been seen that very few new capital intensive factories have come up in last three to four years in Bangladesh as government has stopped giving new gas connections due to drop is gas pressure and no new gas fields have been explored or found. Making electricity available will go a long way in the development of the country by encouraging entrepreneurs to set up projects as this is one thing without which industry cannot run.

Another very important thing for industry is availability of raw materials. There should be clear laws and policies about procurement of raw materials which should be consistent irrespective of which party comes into power as industry is there for long haul and cannot survive if there is some drastic change in the procurement policy or the pricing policy. For industry which is dependent on raw materials which has to be imported there should be logical duties and import policies should be made easier which will encourage entrepreneurs to set up industries even where raw material is not locally available in many cases. It is quite sad to see that we have a huge trade deficit with China, which is mostly importing raw materials from us like cotton, minerals and ores and in turn manufacturing the goods and exporting to us the finished products.

Law and order of a particular state plays an equally important role in the growth and development of industry. The entrepreneurs will be willing to put up projects where there is good law and order situation and political stability in terms of consistency of policies and easy labor laws. This is another area where Gujarat has been able to convince the business people to invest in the state. Assam is a very good example where hardly any industry has developed due to separatist movements and terrorism which have been there in one or the other form for the last few decades. Another state which has not seen much development for many years is Bihar again due to lack of security. Good news for people of

Bihar is there has been a lot of change in the security condition in the last few years, with people saying that they feel much safer and even women can also move out after dark in at least city like Patna which will go a long way in encouraging people to set up industry there. Take the case of West Bengal where for many years industrialists were skeptical about putting up factories due to labor problems during the rule of Communist party and now scared due to whimsical policies and uncertainty during current government. Any leader can talk to entrepreneurs and invite then to set up industry in their area, but unless the business people feel safe and have surety about consistency of policy and good law & order no one will be ready to put up any projects in that particular area. The saddest part is in many cases you do not need a budget or money for this, like you need for developing infrastructure and generation of power but just the will power and desire to put things into place.

The government has a big role to play especially in a country like India in the area of skill development. Our education system as discussed earlier is more theory oriented and not tuned to job requirement so availability of skilled personnel is poor.

We will find that every year there are lots of graduates and masters who are coming out but due to the system of education whereby there is focus on theoretical knowledge and subjects not being tuned to what is actually required in the industry, neither the industry gets people who could be absorbed into the organization nor do the students find it easy to get jobs after they pass out from colleges. Leave apart general graduates, even students who pass out from Engineering colleges apart from small percentage of good institutes get half cooked theoretical knowledge, whereby the curriculum is not in tune with requirements of the industry due to which there is big dearth of productive and skilled man power. The Education ministry has a big role to play here as there is a requirement to review the entire method by which education is being imparted in our country to make it more in tune with what is required by industry whether it is manufacturing or service industry. As mentioned earlier the government has to play a big role as partners of business. The policy makers should sit with people from the industry and try to understand what is required by the businesses in terms of skill and knowledge of the people so that they can make productive contribution once they complete their education or training Also businesses should be encouraged to be engaged with the educational institutions and work with them to align what is being taught and what is actually expected by the industry.

Let us take the case of tourism industry in our country. Such a vast country as India has less number of foreign tourist visiting every year even when compared to a tiny country like Sri Lanka which is not in Europe or America but our Southern neighbor. Another country which we should compare is the figures of tourists that visit China every year. Our country has been given by nature all kinds of gifts, we have sea, mountains, jungles, coupled with historically interesting monuments and attractions. So what stops India from being one of the hottest spots in the world tourism map. If we analyze we will find that it is the basically the same common factors that restricts the growth of the home grown industries. The first thing which stops tourists from coming to India is the state of law and order leading to sense of safety and security of the people visiting our country. We hear regularly cases of violence against women and cases of cheating which the tourists have to encounter in India. It is almost impossible for a single lady to travel around in our country except for maybe in the cities, where also there is no surety that she will be safe if she goes out at night or to some place which is little offbeat or less frequented. Even people who come with families have to be careful about where they going, with whom they are going as there are lot of instances of cheating and security issues. Another reason is lack of availability of good reasonable hotels. There are mostly two categories either the top end four or five star hotels which are not affordable for all or smaller places which lack both the basic amenities and cleanliness. The condition of roads and traffic situation is another deterrent which keeps away a lot of tourists. Though we have seen a big improvement in roads as compared to say 15-20 years back, but still if someone compares it to even China we are still far behind, especially when one travels to places which are away from the main cities. Road conditions coupled with traffic sense and congestion and also availability of good, reliable and affordable public transport system are some of the basic and common reasons which keep tourists away from taking the trouble of visiting our country. The tourists have to either travel by plane or hire private vehicles if they have not come in a group. In most of the cases they cannot think of travelling by bus or train which is what is most affordable when one is touring a foreign country. Also the way the tourists places and monuments are being maintained and the facilities available in these places keeps away a lots of tourists. Let us the take the case of North East India. It is a lovely place with a lot of opportunity to develop the tourism industry creating a vibrant economy and also lot of jobs like Kaziranga and Manas in Assam, Shillong in Meghalaya, Tawang in Arunachal Pradesh just to name a few. But due to security issue combined with non availability of good roads and hotels, maybe not even 10 percent of the potential of the tourists has been tapped till now.

Government will have to focus on the improvement of the public transport system, which will improve the mobility of the people and also make it easier and faster to move goods from one place to another. It will make the work force more productive and at the same time will help in reducing the problem of traffic on the roads. If good and reliable public transport is available to the people many people who can afford a car will prefer to use it only when going out with family or when absolutely required as will save money as well as time. Also more importantly will allow the person to be much fresher when he reaches his office in the morning or his home in the evening. As said the other benefit of this will be lesser traffic on the road allowing the communication to be faster. It will also reduce the consumption of fuel in a big way which occurs due to jams where vehicles are consuming fuel and also causing pollution. The indirect benefit will be reduction in import bill of petroleum and less budget deficit as we are a big importer of oil. It shows that improvement in one sector not only has a direct benefit but a lot of secondary benefits attached to it.

In cities like Mumbai it has to be seen how the sea can be used as an alternative mode for transporting for the working people as it will be much faster and will also reduce the load on the highly congested roads.

Another very important sector which has to be looked into very seriously is healthcare. The minimum healthcare facilities should be available to all sections of the society. Whether is rural area or the under privileged and poor in the urban areas basic healthcare should be ensured for all. It is only a healthy workforce and society that can be productive and contribute to the economy. Government should have hospitals with basic amenities and doctors so that healthcare is available even for the poor and for people for whom private hospitals are not affordable. We have progressed a lot in terms of healthcare available to the people who can afford to pay for it, but this is a small percentage yet of the total population of the country. For the whole country to move forward it has to be ensured that we have a healthy population which can be productive and vibrant. Also the government has to play a big role in educating the population through media and other resources about the diseases like diabetes and how to prevent it. If it is not taken up seriously India could be robbed of the demographic dividend among many other reasons due to diseases like diabetes. At 65 million known cases

India has the second highest population with diabetes. It is not a disease which is caused due to any particular reason but is mostly related to lifestyle of a person and so much more easier to prevent With proper and increased awareness about lifestyle changes like physical activity and a healthier diet this can be tackled to large extent.

With an ever increasing population which is expected to surpass China by 2025 making India the most populous country in the globe government has to think how it is going to accommodate so many people. Are we going to have more cities like Mumbai where 50 percent of the population stay in slums or we are going to have more live able places. Here the government has a big role to play in terms of taking the initiative to develop smaller well planned more live able cities around the country with all the facilities so that people do not flock to places like Mumbai, Delhi or Bangalore only for better chances of earning a livelihood. These new cities should be attractive to the entrepreneurs and the business houses to set up new businesses due to lower costs like the price of real estate so that they not only set up new operations but also move some of their existing business to the new places. This way not only there will be development in different parts of the country, it will be able to bring in more people into the productive cycle and earn a livelihood without them having to move far from their existing places, and at the same time reduce the stress and the resources of the bigger cities making them more habitable and also improve the quality of life of the people staying in these mega cities.

Another very important area to be looked into is the security and empowerment of women. Women constitute almost 50 percent of the society and if majority of this 50 percent is not secure or empowered how the country can progress as a whole. Here only government cannot do much unless the society as a whole does not change the way they look at women. When majority of the women is not productive or have the right to choose what they want to do and have to be at the mercy of what elders and especially the males decide, society is basically loosing almost half of its productive workforce. It is very sad that in today's date also women is looked at an object which can be used as the males want. It is this mindset which leads to social evils like dowry, exploitation and physical and mental harassment of the women. Every day we hear that someone has been raped in one or the other part of the country, and we hear only a small percentage of what actually happens as lot of cases are not reported either due to fear of further harassment or due the stigma which is attached to it. In fact in most of the cases it is the female who is blamed for the crime and it becomes the liability of the victim to prove that something like this has happened to her. Here government has a big role to play. First in ensuring security of the women who dare to come out of their houses to work and study against all odds by not only making laws but ensuring that culprits are given exemplary punishment through a fast track system of justice. There cannot be any bias in this case whether he is the son, brother, cousin, nephew of any politician, industrialist, local don or minor. If these people know that they can get away with it, they will never shy from doing it not once but again and again. In some cases it is the fear which is the only way of preventing crimes and if instilling fear is only way to protect our women from this heinous crime, so be it. It is a shame that Delhi which is the capital of our country is one of the most unsafe place for women. I remember, last year when I was travelling in China and having dinner with a few Chinese guys they commented that Delhi is not only the capital of India but also the rape capital of the world. As touched upon earlier this lack of security and the mindset of the people who do this heinous crime is also responsible and deterrent for tourist to visit our country, as why someone will come to any place for holiday when she is not secured about her safety and even if something happens, there is very little chance of getting justice. It is very shameful to see our politicians saying weird things like the way some girls dress is responsible for rape, or someone else saying guys sometimes make mistake, or pictures of girls being raped and hung in trees and still police either not catching the culprits or not being able to catch them. I am sure if there is sense of fear and knowledge that someone will not go free and will be given the harshest of punishment if they commit this kind of crime almost 90 percent of the incidents will not take place at all. It is the topmost priority of the Central and all State governments to ensure that they can provide security and at the same time make arrangements so that women can feel safe and culprits are brought to justice within shortest possible time. Along with this it is the duty of society and every parent specially the father to teach their son to respect women and look at them not as an object of desire but as equal and someone who gives them birth and hold their hand at every stage of life whether as mother, sister or wife. In this 21st century the crimes and torture that women has to face has to tackled by government and every responsible man in the society.

It will be seen that the things that have been taken up here are common to every place and country in this earth. Those countries that have tackled them better are well off and those that have not been able to do these things so well are lagging behind. Also at the same time these basic things affect each other and usually they move together to make a vibrant, progressing and well to do society. Very soon Brazil is going to host the WORLD CUP 2014. It is a country where football is a religion and people are mad about the game. Every time Brazil plays in the World Cup, the citizens of Brazil expect nothing less that their team to win the competition. In such a case all the people should just be happy that Brazil is hosting the competition this time in their country and do all they can as individuals to make the event a grand success, but even in Brazil we have seen there has been huge protest and demonstrations against holding of the event. This is because the country has spent over 11-15 billion dollars(depending on various estimates which have been reported) for organizing the event and building infrastructure like stadiums and hotels to host the tournament whereas a lot of people though they love the game more than anything else feel that this money could have been much well spent and was in fact essential to be spent for basic essentials like security, healthcare, public transport, infrastructure and education as these are the most basic needs for any people leaving in any part of the world. The dissatisfaction is because people believe that the money that has been spent on building stadiums and other things for the purpose of world cup will be of not much use once the tournament is over and general feeling is that if the same amount of money would have been spent on things like infrastructure, education and healthcare it would have had a long term benefit for a much larger proportion of the population which stay on the wrong side of the economic divide. It is not that people are less enthusiastic about the football world cup or they have stopped loving their football suddenly but it is a question of spending the money in a way which will bring benefit to the people who need it the most and which will have long term effect in terms of improvement in the basic necessities of the people.

A FEW STEPS TOWARDS A BETTER TOMORROW

For a better tomorrow we all as individuals have to strive for change and think what should change for a better tomorrow. I for one feel it has to start from parenting.

We have to see how we are bringing up our child and whether we are giving sufficient time to our child during the early years. What we are showing to them as parents that they will automatically pick up being good observers and fast leaners. We may tell a child that he should do this or do that, or this is right but if they see us not following the same things they definitely will do mostly what they see us do in a particular situation. We cannot expect the child to be disciplined one if we ourselves are not disciplined. No matter what a child is told or taught in school it is what he sees practically that will have the actual impact on what he goes to become as an adult. If a child growing up in a normal urban Indian family see that what their parents and elders talk about is about grades, materialistic possessions like cars, gadgets, bank balance then no matter what he is theoretically taught about values and cultures he will grow into an adult believing in his heart what is important is somehow get good grades, get into a good college, strive to earn a six figure salary so that he can become someone in the society. As parents it is the duty of every parent to first bring discipline in our lives, behave in such a way that our kids can practically see that besides the flashy materialistic possessions there are more important things like respect, compassions, discipline, humanity, religious tolerance, ability to follow your own heart than just be running after some hollow materialistic goal where you will have all the wealth and flashy goods but not the internal fulfillment and sense of tranquility. So it is very much essential for us to first become responsible and conscious parents. We will see that if we can walk the talk, our child will automatically pick up the good things, as they will see practically every day that what we are doing. We have to understand that it is of not much use to try to discipline a child if they see something which is totally opposite to what we say or what is being taught in schools. We have to understand as parents that every child has different capabilities and requirements and adapt ourselves to suit their requirements, and not try to impose our will on the child. We have to let them grow in such a way that they are able to what they want to be and what they like to be. Our role should be just assisting them and guiding them by adapting ourselves as parents by trying to understand each child, rather than forcing them to follow a path that we have designed for them. This way we will bring into the society adults that have an inner satisfaction, who have followed a dream of their own instead of trying to be something with which they do not identify themselves. We have to inculcate in them things like respect for fellow human beings, love, self discipline, ability to judge what is right and what is wrong, create an environment where they feel they have the right to choose and pursue what they enjoy and like. If we want to bring our child to be contended adults we have to focus on ourselves first, we have to understand that we have a very big role to play and have to make a lot of efforts and first understand ourselves and teach ourselves how to create an environment where the child becomes self disciplined. It is the small things what they see their parents do every day that they will automatically pick up and will go a long way in their development into adults. For example if a child see his parents doing some form of exercise everyday he will start to think automatically that this is something which should be done and will pick it up as a part of his routine when he grows up, seeing what a parent actually does make it much easier to bc inculcated in a child than forcing him to do something. If it is boy he looks up to his father and if it is a girl she picks a lot of mannerisms and habits from the mother in the early formative years. A child who sees his parents talks about only money and materialistic things will feel that these are the things which matter the most in life and will strive to achieve these as the goals of his life. When he is not able to get these he will be frustrated and dejected. Till a child goes to school he spends his entire time at home and even after he goes to school he spends a lot of time with his parents and learns from what he sees and what his or her parents does. Imagine a house where a child see his parents, doing some kind some of exercise, reading a newspaper in the morning, parents spending quality time after they are back from work and enjoying the company of each other, respecting each other and discussing things even when they may not have same point of view for certain things, spending quality time in the company of friends and relatives whenever time permits, gives due respect to people whom they deal with, the child will automatically pick up these things as very natural things and do not have to be specially told to these things. On the other hand if he sees that his father does not respect his mother, parents quarrel with each other most of the time, talks only about money and materialistic things, no matter what he has been taught in school and parents tell him the child will pick up in most cases what he see his parents does.

To illustrate how what the parents does, can automatically be picked up kids from an early age I would like to give here an example based on an experiment which was conducted in UK. They put eight monkeys in a room. In the middle of the room there was ladder, leading to a bunch of bananas hanging from a hook on the ceiling. Each time a monkey tries to climb the ladder to get the bananas, all the monkeys are sprayed with ice water which makes them miserable. Soon whenever a monkey attempted to climb the ladder, all the other monkeys not wanting to be sprayed with ice cold water, set upon him and beat him up. Soon none of the eight moneys ever attempts to climb the ladder. Then one of the original monkey is removed and in his place a new monkey is put into the room. Seeing the bananas and the monkeys he first wonders why no one is trying to go for the bananas hanging from the ceiling. But undaunted he immediately starts to climb the ladder. All the other monkeys fall upon him and beat him up. The monkey did not understand why he was beaten up, but he no longer attempts to climb the ladder. Then a second original monkey is removed from the room and replaced by a new monkey. The newcomer again attempts to climb the ladder, but again all the other monkeys fall upon him and beat the crap out of him. This includes the first new monkey, who is grateful that he is not on the receiving end this time, participates in the beating because all the other monkeys were doing so. At the same time he had no idea why he was attacking the new monkey. One by one all the original eight monkeys were replaced. Now there were eight new set of monkeys in the room. None of them were ever sprayed with the ice water, but still none of them attempt to climb the ladder. All of them would enthusiastically beat up any new monkey who tries to climb the ladder without having any idea why. This is how things are imbibed by kids when they see their parents doing the same things day after day.

So parenting is more about educating ourselves and bringing discipline in our lives. We should create an environment where the child learns by watching us rather than being told what to do, and also give space to the child so that he can express and pursue what he likes rather than forcing on to him what we believe is the right way or thing for the child to do. We are bringing up humans who have aspirations, desires, wishes, heart to which they have to listen to, needs that vary from child to child and not dealing with machines that we try to program them in a set way which we feel is the right thing for them to do. If we can do this we will be bringing up adults into the society who have compassion, ability to take their right decisions and most importantly adults who will not be overwhelmed by the dazzle and glitz which they will see around them and try to run after it as the sole aim. Bringing up the child in the right way will solve a lot of the social problems in the society automatically, so as parents it is our utmost duty to learn ourselves first how to bring up our child so that they become responsible citizens, who learns to love themselves and grow up to follow a life which gives then satisfaction and joy in what they are doing with their life. It is happy individuals which make a happy a family, lot of happy families make a happy society and happy and vibrant nation, a nation where individuals take pride in what they are doing. For a vibrant, progressing nation it is very important that the common citizens and the government with its different organizations both play positive roles in every sphere of life as they are like the two hands which need to come together to get a clap. A nation where its citizens are not hard working, do not have pride in what they are doing, have sense of responsibility and discipline will not progress no matter how honest and forward looking its government is and vice versa. The best example to my mind where we can see this is Germany, where the individuals are hard working, disciplined, take a pride in what they are doing, and also have a government which works always for the betterment of the country led by a very efficient leader in Ms Angela Merkel. No wonder that it was one country which could come out of the last economic crisis first among the developed nations and took along with it the whole of Europe so that the other countries did not collapse. It is evident in every sphere of life how a country with a vibrant and proud citizens make it a leading nation in the world for others to emulate. It shows in the fact that it is the biggest economy by far in Europe, any product that they make be it automobiles, textile machinery, industrial equipments, it is of top quality. Being from the textile industry I would like to illustrate it by giving an example related to some textile machines. We were in a textile machinery fair called ITEMA, which is in fact the biggest and the most widely visited textile machinery fair in the world. Just out of curiosity we went into the stall of a German loom manufacturer, (looms are the machines which are used to make fabric/cloth)Dornier, though we knew very well that we could afford to buy these looms. We were in negotiation with other European suppliers at that time for our factory which were in the range of 40,000 euros. When we enquired about the price of the Dornier looms we were quoted price of 80,000 euros. When we wanted to know why such a big price difference apart from the versatility of looms which we knew, the sales guy said that they still making all parts of the loom in Germany and they could give a guarantee that except of the normal consumable items we would not have to buy any spares for the period of 10 years, which is unimaginable for any other brand even from Europe. Even in sports if we take the case of football which is the most popular and widely viewed sports all around the globe it will be seen that they may not have big stars in the team, but come a major tournament like the World Cup they will come out as a team with determination and always find ways to give a good result, like in the World Cup of 2004, when nobody gave them any chance but still they played the finals and were beaten by a very good Brazil team.

On the other hand if we look at the African teams we will find that they always have teams with players with good individual skills and reputations playing in top European football clubs, but when they come to the world cup, they have never been able to perform up to the expectations and best performance till date has been quarter final appearances in the premier football tournament. So what is lacking is the fierce desire to win as in the German teams and also lack of team spirit and discipline, which was amply illustrated by two Cameroon players in the 2014 World cup fighting on the field and one almost head butting his team mate in the match against Croatia.

For any country to progress and the world to be a better place, it is not enough for only that country to do well. In today's world where things are so much interconnected and linked one country is dependent on the other. It is same as family cannot be good and happy one if one member of the family has a problem, or like one family in a neighborhood can spoil the atmosphere of the whole neighborhood. The best example is the financial crisis that happened in the last decade due to subprime loans and too much greed in the financial sector which helped create the crisis. Today in the interconnected financial world problem originating in one place has the capacity to take down with it the entire world financial structure, which is a very scary thing to imagine, especially if the crisis happens in US, or China or Germany. So it is the duty of lawmakers in every country to see how to protect the financial system and take steps to bring in checks and balances into the operations of the financial institutions and banks so that the greed and carelessness of few individuals do not ruin the entire system. There are many forums and conferences/meetings where the world leaders and economists have agreed that the world's largest banks are still "Too Big To Fail". There have been books written about it. In fact IMF chief Christine Lagard has urged for this issue to be tackled and a workable solution should be found at the earliest possible. There have been many who have accused the bankers of trying to block and obstruct important reforms which are necessary to make the system safer. It is these banks which almost brought the entire financial system crashing down and had to bailed out with taxpayers money which play a major role in the policy making and try to block any reforms which may restrict their freedom of operation, but will bring some safety into the system so that their greed and foolishness do not give nightmares to millions of ordinary people. Ms Lagarde has said that people in the financial sector who want to bend the rules will always try to find creative ways of doing so, there is a need to change the culture of the banking industry. And she is very true and correct as unless the culture of greed and incentive linked to higher turnovers and numbers (though not necessarily actual bottom line) is changed people will always try to find means and ways to bend the rules for their own personal gain putting millions of others at risk. It is very sad and scary to see that there has been mainly superficial changes after the financial crisis, but not much fundamental changes in the culture and the system after the crisis. So the world is at risk and have not taken adequate and meaningful lessons from the crisis to avoid a similar situation from happening in the future. Everyone has gone back to their own business, as if things have been taken care of, we see the stock markets in every major country crossing even the highs of when the crisis had started and unless there are fundamental changes in the culture of how the banks and financial institutions operate, backed by adequate checks and balances bought into the system we are surely awaiting for another disaster to happen, and this time we may not be as lucky as the last time. The industry still puts great value and awards short term profits over long term safety and prudence, and on how individuals can earn their next big fat bonuses than on long term relationship with clients and partners. It is very sad that the very people who were responsible for the crisis not only made a lot of money before it but are still being compensated very well even after the crisis and the general people and taxpayers had to foot in the bill. The lawmakers from every country has to really deliberate and find ways by which they can take care of this current situation of Too Big To Fail". They have to find out ways to ensure and see how the system can be protected without severe danger and disruption even if some of these big banks fail, and has to protect the general public and not use taxpayers money to bail out these banks. The whole sector has to bring in fundamental changes and find ways to bring in greater integrity and accountability whereby more importance is put on long term results without putting the institutions and the system into risks. Here also it will be seen that it is the culture and way individuals have been brought up in today's world where they have seen that it is the money and glitz which is the ultimate goal in life that is responsible for looking into the short term gains and try to achieve results that will earn them fat bonuses without any consideration and guilt for the risks they are taking to achieve these short term gains. So besides the lawmakers making laws and systems to bring checks and balances into the system, finding ways to see how to tackle the problem of "Too big to fail", monitor the financial institutions in a way where loopholes can be identified at the much earlier stage, it is also important to have a serious look at the role played by the people high up in the financial sector in terms of social consciousness, responsibility and accountability that will become a cultural change in the long term in the way people in the financial sector does their business.

One of the ways to change this is that employees in banks and financial industry should be rewarded and fined as per medium and long term performance instead of short term results. Whenever a senior executive joins a company he is never asked to prove his faith in the company or his allegiance to the company. How to ascertain what is the stake of the new employee who has joined in the company or the customers that he manages. Does he invest any of his own money, just to show that he has confidence in what he is doing? The way it goes these days any employee joining in a senior position in a bank or any financial institution is given a fat package and built in bonuses based on short term results and performance and also a severance is included in the contract worth in millions in case he is asked to leave for any reason. In fact these bonuses based on short term results is a big incentive for the CEOs and the top executives to take decisions that may look profitable in the short time and also boost the stock prices in the short term, but can have disastrous results in the medium to short term. I think that pay packages and bonuses for the CEOs and top executives who take such vital decisions should be designed in such a way they are bound to take decisions and work like business owners, taking into consideration how it will impact the long term results of the company keeping in view also the relationships they build with suppliers and customers who are in fact partners in the business and play a very important role in the operations of any organization.

Also it is to be seen what is the role of the Rating Agencies, who are giving ratings to the companies, banks and financial institutions. The leaders, think tanks and government in all countries should have some kind of monitoring of the rating agencies. It has to be seen what is the responsibility of the Rating Agencies and to whom they are responsible. There has to be some kind of mechanism to monitor the sanctity of the ratings and ensure that they have not been bought over as ultimately it is only humans who are driven by money that are rating the companies. The role these agencies play in today's scenario is very important and what rating is given by a certain well recognized Rating Agency can change the entire scenario and affect how the company does in the stock market and how their stock prices move in the market.

Anyways where there is lot of authority with very less accountability, there is always a chance of going out of line.

Another very important factor which has to looked at very seriously in our country and as a whole for the world is inequality among the people. It is this inequality and huge difference of wealth among people that is one of the major reason for a lot of the social problems. This ever increasing divide between the rich and poor is in fact a matter of great concern for all the countries. In India whereas the number of billionaires are going up every year still more than a third of the population lives below the poverty line and cannot even afford one proper meal during the day. There are still farmers who commit suicide for not been able to pay back the loan once they have one bad crop due to shortage of rainfall or any other natural disaster like a cyclone. The government in all countries, more so in a country like India has to find ways for better and more sustainable distribution of wealth.

In a country like America it is 1% of the population which holds more than 90 percent of the wealth. The story will be not be much different in India and most of the countries, with maybe few exceptions like the Scandinavian countries. The gulf between the salary of the senior executives and the mean salary is ever increasing thereby increasing the difference in distribution of income. So much difference between packages of the top executives and the other employees brings in dissatisfaction and shows as if the CEO is the only person responsible for the performance of the company. In reality nothing can be further away from the truth. It is always a team work and for any company to perform well all the employees have to make contribution in their own field no matter how small the job may be. I run a textile mill where any subsequent process is dependent on the earlier process being done well, so I can realize how important a role each person plays in the final outcome. Just for example if the operators who are responsible for running the looms are not efficient and dedicated no matter how well all other departments are performing there will be defects in the fabric and ultimate delivery of the fabric will be less. Again say while the dyeing process of the yarn is going on, if the operator running the machine makes a small error in any of the ten steps involved, then the final shade will not come right and all the subsequent processes will be held up causing the total chain of operations to get delayed.

It is said that in today's world it is survival of the fittest or in some cases that in capitalist society those who have wealth deserves it as they have taken the risk and found ways to make their fortune. But it is time to look at the things from a different perspective. There has to be some way to ensure a more even distribution of wealth, whereby yes the people who take the risks, innovate, lead still have the incentive to keep doing their good work but there is a mechanism by which the other people get a bigger share of the wealth generated so that at the end the distribution and holding of wealth is not so skewed in favor of the small minority of the population. The lawmakers and society as a whole as to find out some way so the earnings and distribution of the wealth generated is more acceptable. Also it is to be seen and debated that people who take the risk and the lead in generating wealth have the right to earn more as they are the one who are in fact responsible for the generation of the wealth, say for example if a business person has started a factory which employs 1000 people has in fact facilitated and created the opportunity for those 1000 people to earn a living without which these people would not even have this earning source. Yes the person who started the business and the people in management should earn much more than the other people but, at the same time it should not be so skewed that of the total earning 90% is being enjoyed by 5-10% of the organization and rest small 10% is being given to the majority of the people as salary. It is not that this 5% people who run the business can do so without the contribution, efforts and hard work of the rest 95% of the people, so why not have a system where distribution of the income is more socially acceptable and everyone in the organization feels happy and part of the company giving their best efforts from their heart so that the company can perform even more better. In many cases like in the banks and financial institutions even this logic of more earning due to risk taken does not hold up at all. In fact it is the other way round. If we just go back to the financial crisis of the last decade, it is the unjust correlation and sharing of risk and reward which is not justifiable in any way, which not only brings inequality but also the entire financial system is being put on tenterhook – more importantly it has a corrosive effect on the social fabric as finance is the most important part of the social fabric and society relies on it very heavily.

It will be seen and no matter whether the country has growth or not, whether the company or the bank is making more profit or in some cases loss, the salary of the chief executives does not go down, in fact US bosses are making on average 257 times the average workers salary according to Associated Press /Equilar study published in Independent newspaper. Feel that it is high time that the people who matter and who has taken the responsibility on behalf of the general population by being elected to represent them and make policies should sincerely work towards finding ways to develop a more trustworthy version of capitalism which will enable to reverse the trend of having a more and more unequal society. They have to find a workable way to have a more equal distribution of incomes, opportunity and fairness across all sections of the society. There has to be some way of putting a limit to what the bosses and the risk takers in the financial sectors can earn, and also devise ways to tackle the phenomenon of "too big to fail", so that instead of the lucky few collective prosperity can be made possible. The bonus structure in banks, financial institutions and the big organizations have to be reviewed and changed to bring in more prudence and ways have to be found to co- relate risk taking with responsibility whereby focus is on long term relationship and long term rewards instead of risk without any liability and short term gains. There have been people like many Central Bank governors of the different countries, IMF chief, economists who recognizes and also have been talking about this inequality of income and its catastrophic effect on the society as a whole. They have been speaking about making inclusive form of capitalism, wherein the system of taxation will be more in tune with earnings among different strata of the society, make use of other forms of taxes like wealth tax, property tax, etc so that the income generated or collected through different forms of direct and indirect taxes can then be redistributed in the form of higher spending on basic needs like health, education, sanitation, security at minimum costs for the benefit of the people who cannot afford these on their own.

Not only this the excess money generated can be allocated for the development of infrastructure and new projects like power generation which will in turn lead to growth of the country generating more money and employment opportunities.

By this not only the inequality of income will be lowered to some extent but at the same time society as a whole will be benefitted and there will much less dissatisfaction leading to automatically solving some of the major social problems as when the basic needs of the people are taken care of and they can see that there are possibilities and opportunities for people in the lower income group also to come up in the society through legal means they will not go for antisocial activities, which in turn will improve the security and general law and order situation of a particular place or country. This in return will improve the growth prospects of the country by making it a very attractive destination for local and foreign investments, increase the inflow of people coming for business and with it also bring in higher number of tourists. When the law and order situation is better, another indirect benefit is less spending on security and police as you need a much smaller force to maintain the security and also government can afford to pay lesser number of people a much better salary thereby again reducing the gap of income and also expect the police and people responsible for maintaining the law and order to be more honest and hardworking. So if we look at it bridging this inequality of income has the potential to solve a lot of social problems and also uplifting the condition of the people in the lower strata of the society. The lawmakers, economists and politicians should put their thoughts and idea on how to bridge the monetary and wealth gap between the super rich and the others and find ways to reduce the ever growing inequality of wealth, else it is going to be one of the biggest social problems in years to come as inequality and poverty leads to dissatisfaction and apathy pushing people to do things which they would have never thought they are capable of doing. It could be that there is a totally different income tax slab for the super rich, like people making more than 10 million rupees a year in India. A person who is making more than 10 million a year can definitely pay a higher tax than someone making say 15-20 lakhs a year, say even if he pays 10-15% more income tax than other people he will still be left with much more disposable income than the person making 20 lakhs a year. Other ways could be making the system of wealth tax and property tax more pragmatic, whereby people having assets over a certain amount would be taxed separately as compared to other people. It is the super rich who hold more than 90% wealth in most of the countries and if the lawmakers with economists and other experts can find a logical way of taxing the super rich they should not have much to complain as it will not alter in any way their lifestyle or things they can afford, just that their net worth may look a little thinner than what it is now. In any democratic country any government to come to power, they have to get at least highest number of the total votes casted and unless it is country where there is some kind of law and order disorder or terrorists threats normally 60 percent or above eligible voters casts their votes. So definitely the lawmakers have to work out how they can serve the majority population who have elected them to work for them, rather than make policies and systems which is heavily tilted towards the benefit of a small minority of population most of whom do not even take the trouble of going to the polling center for 1 day in 4/5 years to casts their votes. I am not saying that any kind of policy leaning towards Socialism or Communism could be solution towards reducing the huge inequality as it has already been practiced in many countries in the past and has invariably failed in all the states which adopted it. Definitely there has to incentives for people who are better, who take the risks, who have worked harder, who are leaders have to be rewarded for their superior contribution and achievements, but at the same time I am sure that if the lawmakers and experts work diligently keeping in mind the well- being of all the people instead of being influenced by the super rich, they will definitely finds ways by which the incentive to work harder, innovate and progress is there but at the same time the distribution of wealth in the society is more even as compared to the current situation.

Another important factor which is very important for every country and specially India is the relationship with neighbors and also the relationship with other important countries in the world. Like good neighbors are essential for any family or individual same way it is for any country. If there is unrest in any neighboring country we will see that there is effect of it on the neighbor. A very good example will be the case of ULFA (a separatist organization in Assam). The top brass of the organization had fled to some of the neighboring countries like Burma and Bangladesh when security forces had started their operation in Assam. They had used Bangladesh as a safe heaven and had been directing all their operations from here and had used the country as the transit route for sending arms and ammunition to the cadres in Assam. During one of the operations in which they were trying to send ten truck loads of arms and ammunition, the consignment was caught at the Chittagong port, despite the best efforts of vested interests of some of the people in government and the intelligence. After the change of government, the new government handed over most of the top leaders of the organization to India and have not allowed the country to be used directly or indirectly by the organization allowing India to spend much less resources for fighting and controlling the ULFA. India is a country which has neighbors that share land borders with us on the three sides and though Sri Lanka is separated from the mainland, the distance from the southern states is not very significant. Imagine a situation where each country like Nepal, Pakistan, Bangladesh, China supporting subversive activities against the country. In that case the government will have to use most of its resources and time in trying to contain these subversive activities rather than working on things for the improvement of the country because resources no matter how big a country is never endless. Imagine a situation where India has to be on guard on every front, like they have to be with possibility of terrorist attack originating from Pakistan. The Mumbai attack will always be fresh in everyone's mind when the city was brought to a standstill by a few terrorists who had a co-ordinated and detailed plan to cause maximum damage with direct or indirect support from the intelligence of one of our neighbors. So it is very important that India gives due importance and develops good working relationships with its neighbors, yes the situation with Pakistan is a bit complicated due to the desire of their intelligence service to keep the animosity alive and also their government to keep alive the Kashmir issue as helps in diverting the attention of the people there from real problems in the country, still all efforts has to be made to engage Pakistan also and see how to make them see the point that this conflict is ultimately causing them more damage than it is affecting India. As for the other neighboring countries India has to give them confidence and also show it with actual action on the ground that it wants to work together with these countries as partners and not as big brother so that everyone is benefitted from the relationship and mutual exchange of resources, goods & services, expertise, knowledge and a peaceful co existence. It should be economic and development issues which should be the priority during exchanges between the dignitaries of the countries, which could help bring growth and prosperity to the entire region, so that people in all these countries have a better and friendly co existence. Growth and better economic situation of the people in the neighboring countries will enable India to divert a part of the resources which they have to use for intelligence and security threats originating from these countries. It will also solve issues like migration from neighboring countries and also the threat of these countries being used as the base for terrorist and unlawful activities. Pakistan which allowed its land and the intelligence services for training and arming of Mujahedeen and Talibans to fight against the Russians in Afghanistan can now see how the same thing has now turned into a Frankenstein which is holding to ransom the whole country and has become the biggest threat to the law & order situation and security of the country. Not only the foreigners are shying away from business and trade leave alone investments in that country, but even their own people are trying to shift where ever there are opportunity to shift part of their business to middle east or Bangladesh specially in the textiles. The country needs electricity for home and industry, roads, infrastructure, but a huge portion of the budget is eaten up by spending on maintaining security and buying arms and ammunition for a proxy silent war against India. I am sure there cannot be a better time for India to engage in meaningful dialogue with even Pakistan now as sure the government and also the army there should be realizing by now that it is for good of their own country that they should stop allowing their land for training and arming of the terrorists and anti social elements. India has to convince the people who matter in that country that it is sincere in its commitment and desire to have a mutually beneficial neighborly co-existence with Pakistan, where trade, business, growth, security, mutual exchanges should be the priority and other non relevant issues in today's context should take a back seat. It will not only bring peace to the region but will also allow the government in all these countries to use the huge amount of money they spend on buying arms and ammunition from the western countries in preparation of a war which has no place in today's context to be diverted for other more meaningful purposes like healthcare, education, infrastructure, roads, etc.

In today's world of course it is not enough to maintain only good relation with the neighbors, but also have good working relationships with other economic superpowers and the upcoming economies as trade and business is global and no country can grow and survive in isolation or only with its neighbors. How the government balances its relation with America, still being in the good books of China and Russia so that it can take the benefit of trade and strengths of each country will go a long way in India taking an important role in world stage and benefit economically and help in putting the country on a growth rate of more than 9-10 percent which is absolutely required to create jobs and opportunities for the ever growing population of the country. It is quite a tricky and fine diplomatic balancing requirement to keep America in the good books and still continue to buy oil from someone like Iran. The Indian foreign and commerce ministries will have to work in fine co ordination to enter into mutual trade and business agreements with individual countries and also associations like EU, ASEAN, etc to facilitate trade and business and get benefits like preferential or zero duty, removal of tariff and non tariff barriers, exchange and passing of knowledge and technology. The leaders of the country has to recognize the fact that they will need some countries for acquiring superior technology, some for raw materials and maybe in the coming years some for food security. It is always a fine balancing act how a country goes about it foreign affairs to engage with all the important players

JOINING HANDS TO SURVIVE & PROSPER

For India and the world to be a better place to live in every country on the earth has a big role to play. What happens in one part of the world directly or indirectly affects other part or countries. In some cases like finance the affect is immediately seen as financial world is interconnected and a ripple in one place is immediately felt and show its effect on the interconnected financial world. Take the case of a disease like SARS or EBOLA. Maybe it had started in some part of Africa but any person who has been affected can travel to any part of the world from that country to Europe or America knowingly or unknowingly and the disease could spread. Environmental factors like cutting of the trees or deforestation or even for that matter greenhouse gases emitted will have an effect which may not be visible immediately but will have long term implications not only for that country where the tress have been cut or gases have been emitted into the atmosphere but also for the whole world in years to come in terms of depletion of the ozone layer or El Nino weather conditions. So the need of the hour is for every country to work together and it becomes the responsibility of the richer and developed countries to think seriously how they can work in an inclusive manner so that there is general improvement of condition of the people in every part of the world and awareness is built up in most backward places of the world so that world is a safer and better place for the generations to come. It should not be that the generations which come after 100 years in some of the best places in the world like Scandinavia or

Canada or Australia find that they are not staying in a place which was one of the best places for human beings because their earlier generations could have done much more in terms of helping the poorer nations which could have helped to indirectly make their countries have a sustainable good living conditions. I was very much impressed by the speech of Indian Prime Minister Mr Narendra Modi who said about improving the conditions of the SAARC nations as a whole as this will in long term help not only to make the whole region a better place to live in but also make India a much safer and better country as then the country can use its money and resources not for spending on arms and ammunition for security threats from within the country and from neighbors like Pakistan but could use it for the purpose of development and making infrastructure, producing electricity, making schools and hospitals. America had seen in Sep 2011 how terrorists which stayed in far off places like Afghanistan, coordinated the attack by hijacking three planes and destroying the two iconic buildings of the world at the same time and killing hundreds of people despite all the military might and money the most developed nation spends on security and intelligence to keep their country safe. The richer and the well to do countries have to understand that only way to be safe and secure is when the whole world is a better place and living condition and education of the people in every country improves so that a small minority of people who go ashtray and do not believe in the rules of the society are not able to exploit and motivate a big section of the people to join them in some war which is not going to benefit anyone in the end but will only bring misery and sufferings to their very own people. The developed countries in the world which are making arms and ammunitions and supplying to other countries is indirectly making their own countries unsafe as many of these arms are falling into the wrong hands who are latter going to use some of these to plan an attack through a dirty bomb or some other means. Recently we have seen that America had to finally get involved in Iraq soon after withdrawing its troops from that country and launching airstrikes against the ISIL (or IS) as they like to call themselves. Reports have surfaced that way back in 2012, the US army trained members of the same terrorist group in Jordan. They were being trained by the US instructors for covert operations to destabilize Syrian President Bashar –al- Assad's government. German weekly Der Spiegel confirmed in 2013 that US was still training Syrian rebels in Jordan. These kind of things though look good and something like a master stroke at the time when it is started finally come to bite the very people who had initiated it. The war against terror started by President Bush to make the world a safer place had exactly the opposite effect as evident from the chaotic situation which is prevalent today in Iraq. The pretext for starting the war on Iraq was that it had weapons of mass destruction, though no team who had gone there for inspections had been able to locate any during any of their visits to Iraq. Basically America wanted to overthrow Saddam Hussein and control the huge oil reserves which Iraq had. This so called threat of Saddam was the same person whom America had supported in the nine years Iran and Iraq war, wherein Russia had sold arms and ammunition to Iran and US had sold their weapons to Iraq. The two superpowers of that time made their money by selling weapons to neighboring countries which were at war for nine years without any decisive victor at the end but destroying their economies and bringing misery to thousands of people in these countries for a decade. After years America had two perceived enemies Iran and then Iraq under Saddam who had weapons of mass destruction which could be threat to America. After overthrowing Saddam and loss of many lives of American soldiers finally US decided that they have trained the local army well enough to defend the country and it was time to withdraw their troops from a country which was far from ready to be run without the presence of trained foreign soldiers and had a leader who was not acceptable to majority of the population of the country. The result was swift occupation of large areas of the country by IS fighters who have declared a Caliphate over a big land in Syria and Iraq. These are well trained fighters with advanced arms and ammunition, and the Iraqi forces could not stand up to them when they started capturing one after another town. Definitely Iraq is a much more dangerous place than when Saddam was ruling the country, and the condition of the people is much worse in general. In fact the whole of the Middle East region is a much unsafe place today as compared to when the war on terror was started and the Arab spring began. None of the places have a stable workable government and the economy is struggling in all of these countries. A large portion of land in many of the countries have become breeding ground for home ground terrorists and safe haven for terrorists from different part. What is the change that people in Egypt got after the overthrowing of President Hosni Mubarak. He was a man who was from army and took power and ruled it for long years. But actually was the condition of the people bad during his rule. It had industries, a very vibrant tourism industry and hardly any terrorists mentionable. After his overthrow, the country had elections and Muslim brotherhood with Morsi as leader came to power. There was another movement to overthrow Morsi as people were soon very disillusioned with what he was doing and with an economy showing signs of going nowhere Mr Morsi could not hold on to power for long. The army cracked down on the Muslim Brotherhood putting thousands of supporters including Mr Morsi behind the bars. There was an election from which the Brotherhood was banned from participating and another army chief Mr Sisi has taken over power. So within a very small time the wheel has come full circle. What was gained from all the change and democratic movement, was loss of thousands of lives and an economy which is much worse than when Mubarak was ruling the country and a tourism industry which is almost dead and will take years of peace and stability to come back to its old glory. I myself is one to the people who had planned to visit the country with my family to take a cruise on the famous Nile river and see the Great Pyramids, the Great Sphinx, the Luxor temple, just to name a few. But these will have to wait now and I am not very sure when the time will come when I will feel safe enough to see the land of the great Egyptian Civilization with its great architecture.

Coming close to our country Pakistan gave its land to fighters at the behest of US to train and fight against the Russian occupation of Afghanistan. Also its army and secret service give training and ammunition to the terrorists to fight a proxy war against India motivating them to fight for the liberation of Kashmir. Now these very people whom they had initially trained and encouraged have become Frankenstein. Today despite their best efforts Pakistan is not been able to solve the problem of home grown terrorists, making it one of the most dangerous place in the whole world. There are attacks and bombing not only in smaller places but even cities like Karachi, Lahore and Islamabad are not safe. After an attack on the Sri Lankan cricket team who were brave enough to go there, no team from any country has gone to Pakistan to play any cricket and they play their home series now in the UAE. The government instead of trying to work towards improving the economy and infrastructure have to spend loads of money now on counter terrorist operations, which sadly is showing no signs of reducing in the near future. The most sad incident was the one in which the terrorists entered an army school and fired to kill and injure little innocent kids. The school was targeted mainly because it was an army school and so there would be lot of kids in this school whose parents will be in armed forces. Even after this if the government there and the army just tries to eyewash the people of the country by passing orders whereby they will hang a few terrorists and bomb a few places which are used by the terrorist, it will not have any long term results. The government and the armed forces and specially the intelligence service has to be very sincere and have a long term plan where they recognize that terrorism and subversive activities has no place in the society no matter if these people are working against India or to be used against an Afghan government which could be leaning more towards India than towards Pakistan, because ultimately they cannot be controlled by anyone and one day will they would come back to bite the very people who had promoted them initially.

With so many examples in every part of the world it is high time that countries and developed nations who have more responsibility than other should understand that no unlawful group or organization in any place can be contained or believed to behave in a lawful way and over a period of time these same people who had been trained and provided for a particular purpose will come back to bite the very people who had initially supported it, because by very nature they are unlawful and they have an agenda which is very different from what civilized world thinks and wants. Sales of arms and ammunitions to keep the engines of the industry in your country cannot be justified by putting weapons into the hand of people who will make the whole world unsafe and bring misery to thousands of people in their own country. No country, politician or businessman has the right to endanger the lives of millions of people around the globe by selling weapons to people who will ultimately use it only for their mean reasons. Ultimately these weapons are directly or indirectly going to endanger your lives and the lives of your loved ones.

I am not saying here that countries which are powerful and has the military capability should not interfere at all in other countries. Yes there will be cases which will need the involvement of countries like America, UK, France, for that matter even in some cases China, Russia or India as they have the military strength and capability to engage in very special cases if required. The US invasion of Afghanistan will not be faulted by many as the Taliban was giving the country to be used as a safe haven for Osama bin Laden and his organization and also committing atrocities of all kind to the people of the country, forcing people to accept what they thought was right and running a totally barbaric rule in the country. Also maybe the American bombings during the Bosnian war, where the Serbs were literally wiping out huge Muslim population from parts of the country can be justified and accepted as an intervention where it was required. There have been situations in the past and also will be in the future where the intervention of countries will be required, but these interventions should have the support of the organization like the United Nations and also there should be a general concensus that the situation demands outside intervention and in fact the majority of the people of that particular country or place would like some kind of external intervention. It cannot be based on the intelligence report done by some general or wish of a leader that he wants to get rid of someone because he does not like that person and for some perceived reason thinks him to be a threat to America or say Russia. Every country has the right to defend itself and in such cases where a neighboring country is actually posing a military threat or allowing its land to be used to train and arm terrorists then the threatened country has all the right to use force to neutralize the threat posed to it.

But as mentioned earlier if someone like America or Russia is sending troops to another country then it should not be an unilateral decision, it should have backing of United Nations and most importantly it should be the desire of the majority of the population of the country involved. In that case the troops going in will get the genuine support of the local people which will make their job much easier. Also when foreigners goes into any place they have to respect the people of that place, their customs and beliefs, traditions and try to adopt to their culture which will make them a part of the population. Many a times the existing police and army of the invaded country totally disintegrates, in which case it has to be ensured that a well established local governance with a leader which is acceptable to the majority and an armed force which will include both police and army that is well trained and equipped to handle any kind of internal and external threat has been put into place before America or United Nations forces are taken away from the country. Unless this is ensured there will be big void in terms or security and soon after the foreign troops are recalled there will be groups or terrorists who will take advantage of the situation and will quickly establish their influence, bringing misery to the general population and use it as an opportunity to expand their activities and recruit more people who are disgruntled and disillusioned with the situation. Iraq is a prime example of this situation, where ISIS is expanding at a very rapid rate taking advantage of a leader who is not acceptable to a large portion of the population and also the Americans has left just because Mr Obama had set a deadline for withdrawal of the troops without ensuring that the Iraqi police and troops were equipped enough to handle the threat posed by the situation which was already very volatile, even without the ISIS. With the departure of the US troops Iraq has become very vulnerable and has become a easy target for home grown terrorists as well as the well trained and equipped ISIS fighters. So Iraq is a much more dangerous place then when America invaded it. The country does not have a leader who can keep the country together and it is the breeding place for all kinds of terrorists, with all the infrastructure much worse than what it was and general people definitely are be far worse off than during the time of Saddam.

Also the world has to understand this new organization of well equipped fighters are not a threat to Iraq or Syria alone. It will be a threat to any country like America, UK, France which are perceived by the group as their enemy putting at risk the peace and security of people of the entire globe where they can reach. Maybe America is looking at it as military problem or thinking that there is a military solution to it, but mostly it has been seen that such situations do not always have a military solution. There is a need to have alternative thinking in these situations and the whole civilized world need to work together to have a real solution to the issue. It is not that the people in the organization are all from Iraq and Syria where they have occupied a huge territory under their control. They have been able to motivate people not only from middle east but from diverse places like US, Canada, UK, France of all places. A few youths from India were held at Kolkata who were supposed to leave the country to join the fighters of ISIS. Recently four persons were held in Indonesia who were also on their way to join the organization and have been identified to be from UIGHUR region of China. So this shows that ISIS with its tactics and reach of online communication medium have been able to reach and motivate people from all parts of the world to join them. Firstly the countries of the world have to understand that everyone has a stake in neutralizing these fighters and politics apart all should share information and contribute to see how they can work together to defeat and neutralize these fighters. More importantly there should be a new line of thinking which is beyond military to see what was the root cause for birth of such a strong organization which have more than 30,000 fighters and people from all parts of the globe. What motivates and drives even educated youths to leave their country and families to go to a place where they have no stakes, do not have anyone whom they know to leave everything and fight for something from which ultimately they are not going to get anything. Now some of the people who had gone from different countries to fight for ISIS in Iraq and Syria are going back to their home countries and trying to strike against the people of those countries. One of the incidents which should awaken the whole world is the attack on the satirical publication Charlie Hebedo in Paris where they entered the premises of the publication and killed 10 people. Just after that two persons in Belgium were killed by the security who were planning some kind of terror attack in Brussels. Unless the think tanks in the entire globe try to find the main cause of this they will not be able to get a permanent solution to rise of such organizations in any part of the world where there is vacuum created due to weak government, who do not have the support of the mass people and also not strong to maintain law and order by the use of police and military. No country can think that it a local problem from which it is isolated and they will not be affected by it, specially a vast country like India who shares its borders with so many countries and which has so many diversities.

At the same time politicians and law makers should see what and how much should be allowed in the name of freedom of speech and right to express someone. Is it ok that some newspaper or publication can publish articles or pictures which can hurt the sentiments of people belonging to a particular religion or sect. Yes we love our freedom and the ability to speak our minds but doesn't this also come with responsibility and certain limits. Like there are rules against defaming a person without enough proof and provision where that particular person can sue a newspaper or a publication or a news media if they publish something which is not correct or backed by enough evidence similarly there should be some guidelines about what media can say and write when it could hurt the beliefs and sentiments of the people of a particular religion, sect or community. There has to be tight control and monitoring of leaders or self- styled preachers who promote hatred and give provocative speeches and openly promotes violence and anti- social activities. There cannot be channels who are allowed to run in television broadcasting programme all the time which are giving out speeches and programs that incite violence in the name of religion and which promotes division among different sects and communities by altering the facts and presenting things in a way that encourages hate and urges people to fight against each other in the name of religion. There are many such television channels like these which are running in different places in Middle East. Even in UK there are channels that are allowed to run which promote these kind of division and religious hatred, in the name of freedom of speech. Like teachers and doctors the people in the news media has a responsibility to bring the correct facts to the people without distorting the facts for the sake of popularity and TRP ratings and also at the same time to use their good judgment and avoid things that could incite violence and hatred among people.

Also India and the entire world has to work together to protect the environment and the natural resources so that the generations to come can have a sustainable life on the globe. It is not that these natural resources belong to one country or that any place could isolate itself from the consequences since they are not polluting or destroying the natural resources. Take the case of rivers which sometimes passes through different countries and vast distances. Unless there is a combined effort to protect the rivers by all the countries it will be of no use if one of the countries is doing its best to protect it but others do not put in any effort to protect it and keep it clean. There has to be a concerted effort on part of everyone to think and find ways how we can have a balanced approach to development and also protection of the vital natural resources and environment so that everyone including generations to come can enjoy them and can have a sustainable living on the earth. The rivers are very important natural resource for human race and all other living creatures on this earth and has a big part to play in the ecological balance of the planet earth. When civilizations started one of the main factors that helped people to settle down and start a life whereby they did not have to continuously move from one place to another like the nomads, rivers played a big part. It provided water for irrigation which enabled people to start doing farming and at the same time also provided food in the form of fishes and other water creatures. Later on as man made further progress with the development of iron, wheel, boats, these rivers became the roads for the boats and small water vessels to move from one place to another allowing in the process people a very convenient and easy way to do trading and exchange of goods. If we see all the early civilizations had started by the side of one or the other big rivers like

Nile for Egyptian civilization, Indus for Harappa civilization, Euphrates for the Mesopotamia civilization to name a few. Not only in the early times but later on also if we see we will find that rivers were one of the main reasons for people to settle down and finally leading to the growth and development of big cities, be it Paris by the side of Seine river, London by the side of Thames, New York by side of Hudson, Cairo by the side of Nile, Budapest by the side of river Danube just to take a few names. The rivers used to be the lifeline on which the growth and development of the human mankind depended and still depends and it is duty of all to protect the rivers so that these rivers can continue to provide water that can be used, food in the form of fish and other living species that survive in fresh water and also means of transport for years to come and play its important role in maintaining the equilibrium of the environment. But due to industrialization, lack of initiative and nexus between corrupt business people and officials we can see the degeneration of these rivers especially in the case of the developing and under developed countries. I feel very sorry to see the state of rivers like Turag in Dhaka which once used to the lifeline of the city. Today due to continuous dumping of effluents from different industries and all kinds of wastes that one can think, combined with encroachment by people with officials and politicians giving a blind eye just so that they can make some money which they may never use or need in their lifetime, the river has become a canal in most places and water is so dark and black with pollution that leave alone using the water by human beings for any purpose it cannot sustain any kind of living organisms in it. Few people for their petty gains have killed the river leaving it good for nothing, bringing misery and difficulty to a large number of people who used to depend on the river for water, as well as for their livelihood. I am mentioning the state of Turag river because I pass through that river every day when I go to the factory and see the condition of the once mighty river. A few days during the rainy reason I can see water flowing and maybe the color is light grey due to the flow of fresh rainwater in large volume instead of black which is the color during other times. The story of our mighty Ganges is no different as is the case with most of other rivers in India, China, and other similar countries where people have taken for granted that they can dump anything they want in these rivers and successive politicians, businessmen and officials have given a blind eye to people using these rivers for their petty benefits. Also we as general people have been equally responsible as have used these rivers for dumping all kinds of garbage and wastes making the water un useable in large portion of its flow through the plain of the sub continent before it meets the sea as most rivers do. By destroying and polluting these rivers ultimately we are only harming ourselves and ensuring that generations to come will be cursing us for making the water of these rivers un useable. With the ever increasing population and more and more use of ground water, protecting these rivers are becoming more and more important for survival of humanity. It is said that in future wars will fought for water as we see being fought for oil and other rare natural resources as water is the most essential thing for the survival of any living creatures including plants and animals and if things don't change for the good, availability of water is going to become more and more scare in days to come. I remember during my stay in Ahmedabad from 1996-2002, shortage of water was a big issue. The colony where we used to stay had its own boring for water as there was no supply of water from the municipal corporation in the Satellite area where I used to stay. Due to continuous taking out of ground water in a place where there is not adequate replenishment of the same as there is not much rainfall in Ahmedabad within 3 years we had to go for new boring which was 100 feet deeper than the original boring as water availability had gone down considerably in those 3 years. I can imagine the situation of the people in these areas if water from Narmada would not have been made available to them. It would not have been long when people in these areas would have to depend on water from outside and stand in lines for it. Now we are facing this situation in Bangalore in the apartments that we stay in at Sarjapur Road. There is no municipal water supply in this area. The water requirement is fulfilled by boring water but it is not sufficient so everyday a large percentage of the water is bought from outside, we do not know from where this water comes and what is the quality of water. But there are areas where water is supplied from Kaveri river and we are awaiting the good days when we will also be able to get water from the river Kaveri. The whole point of giving these examples with regard to water situation that I have personally faced is to illustrate what an important role these rivers play in our life and how important it is for everyone including general population to ensure that these rivers are protected, without the dumping of industrial wastes, garbage and illegal encroachments for petty needs. It is not only the rivers but all other water bodies which have to be protected and preserved like the lakes, ponds etc so that the water is not polluted and these can continue to be used for the purpose of the needs for generations to come. It is not only for the water to be used that these water bodies are important, they serve many other purposes like acting as habitat for migratory birds, support and maintain the ecological balance, provide food to humans as well as other living organisms in the form of fish and other water based organisms. They also act as natural reservoirs and can hold a lot of water during heavy rains and prevent sudden flooding as seen happening in most of the cities during one heavy downpour. I know of one city Ahmedabad which used to have a lot of these lakes once upon a time and they used to act as reservoir during rain, and now that they have filled up, the city gets flooded whenever there is a heavy rainfall for few hours as neither there is sufficient drainage for the water to go out nor there are these natural water reservoirs which could take up a lot of the rain water. It is not only protecting and keeping our rivers, lakes, etc clean and intact, but we have to think about innovative ways how we can preserve water and reuse water so that water is available not only for us but for generations to come, find ways to make water available to most of the people for drinking as well for agriculture and industry. The idea should be to find the most judicious ways to use and reuse the water that is available. There is a plan to make water available in Sabarmati river in Ahmedabad throughout the year by supplying treated sewage water, once the availability of water from Narmada may not be possible after the Sardar Sarovar dam's canal network is over. These are the kind of innovative idea and thinking that is required along with the initiative from the government which can ensure preservation of water and at the same time ensure that water is available to larger section of people and throughout the year. There has to be a concerted effort to preserve water and at the same time find ways to make water available as it is required for all kinds of activities from agriculture, to power generation, and also industry. Without WATER life cannot be sustained and it is the most vital requirement not only for survival of the living organisms but also for growth and sustainability. So everyone should be made aware of the importance of preserving the water bodies, avoid wastage, find ways to reuse water and government and public participation is required to find innovative ways to make judicious use of water. Once government in Tamil Nadu had decided that it will implement zero discharge norms for textile industry yes it caused some temporary disruption and some of the smaller factories in places like Tirpur had to close down, but it was a small price to pay to ensure that water is reused by the industry and also they do not cause pollution. Yes it is costly for industry to treat the water by reverse osmosis process, but they can now almost reuse close to 90 percent of the water after treatment and have to top up about 10 percent. Imagine the big impact that it is going to have on the long term, especially for a place like Tamil Nadu which is naturally hot and dry with much less rainfall than many other parts of the country. It should be made compulsory that people have to find ways to do water treatment of sewage water, and also do rain water harvesting especially in the new apartment complexes that come up in the cities and house large number of people in a one complex. Also societies should have meters for every individual apartment to find the use of fresh water and billing should be done according to the actual use of water. This will be the most effective way to prevent the wastage of water as today everyone understand either the language of law (if implemented properly) or the language of money. I am very sure that if water use in monitored by using meters and households are charged accordingly, the wastage of water will go down by 50 percent immediately.

In a country like India which has so much diversity, where there are places which have a lot of rain and some other places where is scanty rain, places which have been blessed with rivers which are perennial and also other places where there are rivers where flow of water is dependent on the rainfall, there has to be ways to make proper use of the water resources that we have so that water can be made available to most parts of the nation which will help in development of all the parts of the country. There was a proposal when Mr Vajpayee was the Prime Minister to link the rivers and there was also study which was done on the river linking project. Yes it could be a project that will run into huge costs and will take a long time to complete, but this is the kind of innovative idea and thinking that is required if the country has to have sustainable growth. Imagine the situation we would still be in if initiative was not taken by the government to build highways during the BJP government under Mr Vajpaee or the telecom network established during the time of Mr Rajeev Gandhi under the able guidance of Mr Sam Pitroda, we would still be going from Bangalore to Hyderabad only by trains as a road journey would have not taken less than 14 hours, and India would never have thought to be the most preferred destination for outsourcing of IT services by countries all around the globe.

If we destroy our rivers, lakes and other water bodies, by pollution and wastes, the day will not be far when we will see that we have industries which are producing all kinds of goods, there has been huge industrial growth, but we do not have the basic necessity for survival as without water nothing will be able to survive on this planet. Along with clean breathable air, water is the most important element for survival of human beings and other forms of life. It is not only the duty of the government but every citizen on the planet to see how the water bodies are protected for our own survival and also for the survival of generations to come. No amount of industrial and economic growth will be of any use without the availability of clean useable water.

Yes government and so called social service organizations have a big role in bringing awareness among the people that preservation of water bodies becomes a MOVEMENT in itself so that everyone is aware and contributes to its preservation and role of monitoring from government agencies becomes much easier and effective.

There is another side and reason also to ensure the protection of the rivers and other fresh water bodies in every part of the globe. When ground water is continously taken out year after year and there is not sufficient replenishment of the ground water then it causes the rock layers below the ground to crumble. In the long run the depletion of the ground water leading to the crumbling of the layers of rocks is causing many cities to slowly sink. It is happening in many parts of the world from Texas in the west to cities in the east like Bangkok and Jakarta where it is so severe that in some places the ground is sinking by up to three inches every year making these places and the people very vulnerable. It will not be too long if this continues when any high waves in the sea will cause floods in these area of the city and any heavy rain even for a short duration will lead to flash floods as water will not flow naturally to the sea as these areas will be below the sea level.

Same is the case with the protection of trees and forests and mountains. The indiscriminate cutting of trees and clearance of forests is having a big effect on the environment. Again it is a case of doing things without much thought about the after affects and greed of the people for making money with the aid of greedy officials who instead of protecting and taking care of these things are making money. Like the water bodies these trees and forests have a very big role in survival of the human race. The trees and plants are converting the carbon dioxide into oxygen without which again life will not be sustainable on this earth and nothing can survive. It is an estimate that a leafy mature tree produce in a day as much oxygen as 10 adults inhale in a year. To produce food the trees absorb carbon dioxide and locks it in the roots and wood beside the leaves acting as a natural sink for carbon dioxide which is considered the main reason for the global warming. The trees also keeps the air clean by absorbing pollutants like carbon monoxide, sulphur dioxide and others and also thereby lowers the air temperature. It is estimated that a place devoid of trees will have a much higher temperature than when compared with a place which has a lot of trees around. I could feel this everyday while coming back from my factory to the city. When I had started working here in Bangladesh eleven years back, the area where the factory is located used to be very green and I had to cross a lush green forest on the way. In summer time I could see that the temperature variation used to be 3-4 degree centigrade between when I started from factory and by the time I used to be in the city. It also acts as natural cleaner of the soil by absorbing chemicals and other pollutants that have entered the soil. The trees also help is fighting the soil erosion by binding the soil by breaking the force of wind and water. It conserves the rain water and reduce the water run offs. The underground water holding aquifier are recharged with the slowing down of the water run offs. They thus act as natural barriers to flash floods. We had seen the huge floods in Uttarakhand recently. It is not that it was the first time the place had such heavy rains but the main difference was it was a place with lot of trees. With the need to accommodate more people due to the ever increasing population and cutting of trees in the name of development without thinking about the implications the water holding capacity and the natural barrier which used to be there due to the trees has been removed so the water does not get any resistance and comes in great force bringing with it the top fertile layer of soil. With the indiscriminate cutting of the trees and clearing of forests for making money and industrialization we are creating a huge disaster for the generations to come. Yes we need development, there has to be industries for which land is required, also with the increasing population land is also required for agriculture, land is required for making houses for the people, sometimes trees has to be cut for the making of roads. But there is always a better way to do things and conserve the trees and forests. Bangalore where I stay used to be a nice lovely city with very pleasant climate around the year, never crossing 30 degree centigrade in the summer. It was not very long, just talking about some 15-16 years back. Today in summer temperature goes up to 40 degrees, as lot of green area have gone and in its places there are big building with glass and steel to accommodate the people working in mostly the IT industry. Yes some amount of temperature rise is maybe inevitable as if we want development and growth we will need to build houses, roads, infrastructure in the cities. But with good planning and with awareness the adverse effects can be reduced to a great extent. For example it can be made compulsory that in every apartment complex or business complex they will need to have this much open area with trees and plants. There has to be some areas in the cities which should be designated as green area where no matter what the trees and plants will not be cut and will be conserved. This will not only keep the air in the cities much cleaner, it will also help in keeping the temperatures down and also reducing the flash floods. These are very simple things which are very easy to implement and maintain, it is just that the politicians, bueruacrats, municipal corporation people have to be little honest and have some forth sightedness. As the scientists are saying the temperature of the earth is increasing with every passing year due to emission of gasses and pollutants into the air causing global warming, which is in turn causing the ice layers to melt leading to rise of the water level in the seas. It is very evident that there are multiple effects due to the pollution that is ever increasing due to the development of industries and the best way that we can reduce the harmful effects is by having more and more trees and conserving our forests as they are the best natural cleaners of the air. By protecting the forests and planting trees, and by ensuring that some areas of the cities are kept and maintained as green areas we will be able to contribute a lot towards the long term preservation of the air which is the single most essential element for survival of life on the earth. If we do not become conscious now and take steps in this direction, very soon most of the cities in the newly developing countries like China and India will be like Shanghai and Delhi where people have difficulty in breathing due to the high amount of pollution in the air due to the vehicles and industries. The situation is so bad that sometimes schools in Beijing have to be closed due to very high pollution Before the Olympics in 2012 in Beijing, they were compelled to close a lot of polluting industries in and around the city so that they could reduce the pollution in the air and athletes could have sufficient oxygen in the air to allow them to be able to participate in the games. When we clearly know the effects of not preserving the environment, then what could be the reason of not taking steps now when it is not too late to preserve the same. It is the duty of the leaders and policy makers to take earnest steps today so that the generations to come do not curse them and they can also have a place where they can have a good quality of life at least not deprived of the basic necessities which is required for survival of people on this earth. These are collective responsibilities of not only the nations where these industries are coming up but all the nations in the world as in the long term it is going to affect everyone.

The role of collective action and prevention is best illustrated by the emergence of Ebola in West Africa recently. It is not that Ebola is a new disease which just came up newly. It has been a disease which has been there on and off since first detected in Uganda and then in places like Congo, Sudan, etc. Since it was never detected in any of the developed countries, no one took any steps to do any research on it or steps to develop medicines or vaccines for this disease as it had not affected any- one except in Africa and putting money behind developing a vaccine for a disease which had occurred in a place where people were very poor to afford the vaccine was maybe thought to be commercially not viable. Another line of thought could be when the disease is confined only to Africa why should we bother about it and devote resources in finding a cure or vaccine for this disease. This time also when the disease was initially detected and confined to places like Guinea, Liberia and Sierra Leone, the WHO and the developed countries had taken a view that it is something occurring in West Africa and there is nothing much to be concerned about. Only when it became serious and started spreading to places like Mali, Senegal, Nigeria and especially when people from Europe and the United States who had gone there for social work or as medical staff got affected, with casualties rising by the day did the developed world started to pay real attention and have put their efforts in finding a cure and vaccine for the virus. In the meantime vital time has been lost and as of now WHO latest report says that almost 10,000 people are being affected on a daily basis. This shows that thinking locally and only about ourselves could be the biggest folly in today's interconnected world where there is free flow of people and goods. The whole world has to take note and countries which have the resources and the capable people with the knowhow like United States, Europe, China, India, Brazil to name the prominent ones have to think globally and contribute towards the common causes so that the world as a whole is a better place to stay in and take steps together so that the local problem is tackled with a global perspective and contained so that it cannot reach a stage that it affects the mankind as a whole. This outbreak of Ebola should be a good learning lesson for the leaders and law makers to think differently and with a new perspective so that in future it does not reoccur. This should be enough to give a wake- up call and initiate a new line of thinking among the world leaders to see how to do much more to find ways and means for prevention of diseases not only in their countries, but to see how to make the world a safer place. What kind of resources the leading nations should devote to see that there are better health care facilities and medicines available in the poorer nations. Also to see what can be done to improve the life and the standard of the people living in backward nations so that such kind of diseases can be prevented from occurring in the first place and how to tackle and nip it in the bud without waiting for long for it to become an epidemic.

Corruption is an area which is prevalent everywhere in the world, yes the level and how much corruption may vary from richer countries to poorer and less developed countries. Otherwise the queen of Spain of all people would not have to step down and face charges of corruption. This has permeated into every part of the society and is one of the major reasons for the problems facing the world. It is this corruption and greed which is exploited by few for their own accumulation of wealth by unfair means which deprives many others and causing harm not only to environment by cutting of trees, filling of rivers and water bodies for making houses and establishments but at the same time is one of the biggest reason for the security threat to the entire world. Countries of the world should come together to think how they can tackle this menace of corruption and co-operate at government level to control it to the maximum possible extent. It is the corruption at different levels and greed which allow the people who are involved in activities like drug trafficking and arms smuggling to carry on their activities. There was a case where in USA one the premier banks like HSBC was fined heavily for transfer of funds which was linked to people in the trade of drug trafficking. Also the people who had committed the terror attack in Mumbai holding the whole city to ransom for days could carry out their act as they were able to enter by bribing the people of coast guard who were there only to protect the country from such incidents. The leaders have to think how to prevent it by enforcement and also think what change in mindset and situation is required to prevent corruption. For example let us take the case of a traffic police who is supposed to check any violation of traffic rules. These traffic police are so poorly paid in a country like India that it is difficult for them to run a family where by they can provide for food, education of kids and a decent life with what they earn legally, so it is very natural that he will let a person who has jumped a red light at a traffic signal to go without any official penalty in lieu of some money which goes into his pocket. So bigger the crime, bigger is the money offered by the criminals and hence bigger the temptation to look the other way. On top of it there are politicians who interfere when someone know to them is caught by police making it a dangerous nexus where money and connections enable the people involved in criminal activities to carry on their acts. I was watching a program in television on Mr Wilson Raj Perumal who used to be involved in fixing football matches. This person was not regretful for what he had done and had taken it as a profession and means to earn his livelihood. He said that it was much easier to corrupt the officials from African nations as FIFA did not pay very well and the many of the officials in the matches coming from Africa did not have a stable job unlike the ones who come from Europe. He said that there was a football tournament which was held in Antalya in Turkey where teams from four nations had participated and all the matches were fixed. He said that among all one particular official from Niger by the name of Ibrahim Chaibu was his favorite whom he had used to fix even some World Cup warm up matches. He even boasted that he had offered one of the officials half a million dollars to fix a match in the World Cup but he was denied. His diary which was found after catching him contained the contact details of a large number of office bearers which were linked to FIFA from different nations.

Another good example to show that world has to work collectively for certain issues is the growth of the terrorist organization called ISIS in Iraq and Syria. As taken up earlier this organization could come into existence due to the void which occurred due to no governance in Iraq and the civil war which started in Syria. Because of its radical and violent ways of going about its operation which was widely covered by media and easy access due to internet, it was able to attract a lot of people from different parts of the world including Europe and North America. People were attracted to its different way of violence and quick and growing influence and started thinking that this could be a very easy way to do something real with their lives. Firstly it was the mistake of United States to pull out their army without ensuring that there is viable government in Iraq and also ensuring a police and armed force which was capable enough to take over once the US troops where pulled out. At the same time the West was also supporting directly or indirectly a civil war with the hope of overthrowing Assad in Syria, again leaving a big territory in Syria where, the government had lost control, making it an ideal ground for the ISIS to fill the void. Once the group captured a vast area in Iraq and Syria declaring a Caliphate of their own the response of the world leaders was more surprising. USA was backing Mr Nuri al Maliki their puppet till the very last and only when realized that he could not in any way manage the country and unite the forces, they stepped to bring about a regime change but by that time a lot of damage had been done and ISIS had taken more ground with every day passing. Again since Mr Obama had made an election campaign promise that he will not have US forces on the ground in Iraq, they are still with the hope that the disorganized Iraqi army will be able to somehow contain the jihadists with some kind of air support. Similarly in parts of Syria they are hoping that Kurdish forces will be able to resist the ISIS with weapons and personnel much inferior to the forces they are fighting. Why cannot the world forces under the umbrella of the United Nations come together and find a common ground to fight the ISIS. Turkey an US ally does not want to get involved in the conflict even though the ISIS jihadists are fighting a war for getting control of Kobane a place which is on the border of Turkey. Just very recently after a lot of time Turkey has said that they would allow some Kurdish Peshmerga fighters to cross into Kobane through its territory as reinforcement to the Kurdish fighters who have been holding their ground with their limited weapons and personnel. Yes Turkey has a long standing conflict with PKK, but does it think that the ISIS, will be happy by capturing the Syrian town of Kobane and will not move beyond as Turkey is too powerful or they have come to some kind of agreement that they will limit themselves to only Iraq and Syria. ISIS is a threat to everyone, it has no ideology as such beyond expanding their influence and destroying whatever the world believes in. So why cannot the countries like United States which considers itself the protector of world order along with the other countries come to a common ground to interfere immediately with whatever forces required to ensure that these ISIS forces are defeated and show that when it comes to peace and security the civilized world will come together to defeat the forces of destruction and terror. There is now a more logical and genuine reason for the United States, Britain and others to get engaged there than when they decided to send their forces to Iraq looking for weapons of mass destruction which was not there from the very beginning.

It is of utmost importance that nations of the world come together and co-operate with each other against the fight against online hacking and terrorism. Any information on terror suspects should be shared among the civilized world so that they know they are against an united world. Just as an example the two Kouchi brothers who were responsible for the attack on the satirical publication in Paris were on the no fly list of both America and the UK, but was this information shared with the French security force. Here the French intelligence is also at big fault as both the brothers were suspects and had served jail sentences in past and had travelled many a times to Yemen, so how they could afford to drop them out of the radar totally and not keep a much closer watch on them. There should be regular flow of information and intelligence among the different nations when it comes to people who could be danger to lives of the people, without only thinking about themselves as these people will one day strike against your country also. The same is the case with people who are suspects of online hacking. Like for people who spread hatred and terror the people who do online criminal activities and hacking will also harm your own nation and can cause mayhem by disrupting anything which is working based on internet. They should be continuously tracked and treated as any other criminals as they can strike anywhere in the world crippling the most sophisticated systems like in a bank or an airline traffic guiding system causing even more actual damage in terms of financial loss and loss to human lives.

So it is very obvious that it is high time to accept and realize that world is inter-connected, no one is isolated and any event in any part of the world is going to have an effect in short or long term on the other part of the world. It is high time that the leading nations and the leaders start thinking in long term with a global perspective. In today's world no nation can have unilateral military dominance and establish their rule like in the earlier days when England had such a vast empire that it was said the "Sun never sets in the British Empire". Today with nuclear weapons in the hands of nations like Pakistan the world is a very dangerous place. One weapon of mass destruction falling in the hands of the terrorists could cause unimaginable damage to the human mankind. It is high time world leaders instead of thinking of how to maintain their influence think how to work together so that world is a safer and better place. It is for the betterment of everyone if all countries develop and poverty is reduced universally, as it will reduce resentment and there will be lesser breeding ground for dissatisfaction and people like Osama bin Laden and organization like ISIS to motivate people to join them for mindless killing and violence. The countries like United States, China, India which source a lot of their raw materials and resources from say Africa has a big role to play to see that their thinking is not limited to exploit these countries and somehow get their requirements by greasing the palms and bribing the leaders and officials, but devise a mechanism whereby the benefits of the earnings percolates down to the people of these countries so that with time more and more people come out of poverty and into the mainstream of society.

With development and reduced poverty, there will be less breeding ground for people to be manipulated, there will be less chances of diseases, with education people in these areas will learn about the benefits of family planning, which will result in slower growth rate of the population which in return will put less stress on the resources available in these less developed parts of the world. A more affluent and educated population will be more aware of the benefits of protecting the environment and reducing the pollution and also protecting the natural resources. There can be no reason why there is poverty in the delta region of Niger river which accounts for almost all of the oil produced in the country. The main reason for terrorism in this area is the exploitation of the people and not proper distribution of the wealth earned by exploration of oil from this area. The oil is being explored by mostly foreign companies and the benefits go to these oil companies and the higher officials in the government and maybe some local leaders and strongmen. Why not think in an alternative way, say collectively these oil companies and the government decide that certain percentage of the earnings which comes from the oil exploration from this region will compulsorily go towards the development of this region. These oil companies are spending huge amount to money for security and also maybe as ransom whenever some of their people are being abducted by the terrorists, also many a time there is disruption in their work due to terrorist attacks. Why not think differently and divert this money for the development of the region. They have huge clout with the governments in these places as without their expertise it would not be possible to bring out the oil. Why not use this clout constructively and think long term and even come to an agreement with the government whereby dictating that a certain percentage of the earnings from the oil and gas has to go for the regional development, uplifting the life of the people. They can build roads, hospitals, educational centers, vocational training institutes, land development where people can have ready places to start up business and industries. It will make the region a safe place where these companies can then conduct their business without disruptions and spending huge amounts of money on security.

Another case which can illustrate the benefits of development of the poorer regions is the case of huge number of migrations from Africa into European countries like France and Italy and then into UK and other European countries. There are huge number of people from Africa which try to enter Europe by any means, including risking their lives by taking small boats overloaded with people to find a better way of living. Since they do not see any future in their own countries they risk everything leaving behind friends and families, the place they grew up in and the environment they have known since birth just to escape the situation of no hope and enter into Europe by any means in the hope of a new and better life. These people come in small boats with children across the Mediterranean sea and mostly rescued by Italian navy and end up in a place called Calle. There they survive on food given by aid agency in makeshift tents and await their chance to move into other countries like Britain. Last year more than 400 people died in the Mediterranean while trying to make one of these voyages to the land of their hope. Same is the case with people from Indonesia who risks everything to reach and somehow find asylum in Australia. Or take the case of people from Mexico and other Central American countries who leave no stone unturned to somehow enter into the United States to find a life which will enable them to make a decent earning staying illegally and taking the risk of being deported if caught. I am sure if these people would see even some chance of earning a livelihood and hope for the future in their country they would never take these risks and at the same time lead a life of illegal immigrant, leading a life of no self- respect. These illegal immigrants are not only putting further strain on the resources of the countries where they end up but also pose a security and law and order problem for that place. People who do not have anything and with an empty stomach can go to any length to survive as they have nothing to loose. The accumulation of wealth among a few nations and more so in the hands of the very small percentage of population in these developed nations and even smaller miniscule portion of people in the backward nations is one of the root cause of lot of problem in the world. A little better distribution of the wealth will go a long way in uplifting the lives of a lot of people and solve a lot of the problems for the world as a whole. If people see a future and hope in their own countries they will never take the risks to illegally migrate to the wealthier nations to find livelihood. It is in the interest of the wealthier nations to sit together and see what they can do constructively to improve the condition of the people in the poorer nations.

Even in terms of economy I see that the leaders of the different nations should look at the world as a place which is highly interconnected and only thinking about what is happening in their country is not enough or something like shutting the economy to say protect their industry or business is not a solution any more. Yes definitely they have to give priority to decisions and making policies which will ensure growth of their economy and keep their industry employing their people running but this also have to be done keeping in perspective what is happening in other parts of the globe. Now take the case of China who is considered the factory of the World, whereby they are producing a huge percentage of the goods like textiles, leather, toys, lower to medium end electronics and supplying it cheap. The West is consuming it and the cheaper prices means many of the businesses in these areas have closed down in the West and have moved to some other places including China. Now let us assume the West comes up with something very drastic like putting tariff and non- tariff barriers to prevent China from exporting some of their goods to their countries. It is not that the slowdown in the economy in China will affect China alone, but this slowdown is going to have an impact on the entire globe. Maybe with its huge reserves China will still be able to sustain itself for quite a long period of time but for the West with a very high debt economy dependent on more borrowings it will be a bigger disaster. So in today's interconnected world the leaders have to think and find a way how to keep the engines of growth running together. The trick is in each country finding its own niche and progressing together so that the entire economy in the globe is able to maintain sustainable growth. The leaders and nations have to find out how their countries and the people can adapt to keep the engines of growth running. Just for an example Germany has been able to show that it is possible to be a major producer and exporter of heavy industrial products despite the high labor costs as compared to China or India or even in most cases the nations in the Western world.

Similarly maybe France can find its niche in the wine and fashion industry or Italy in high end textiles and top end leather and garments. Bangladesh is a very small country and one of the most backward countries with hardly an economy say 20 years back. Even without much contribution from the government or policy makers just by the efforts and determination of the entrepreneurs the country has been able to find a niche in making of garments using the pool of hard working female population and after China is the second biggest exporter of garments in the world.

All the above shows very clearly if that the leaders and law makers start thinking of the globe as one big nation and work out how to improve the conditions of the people in the backward countries and also the underprivileged in their country it can have huge impact on the conditions of living of the people in every part of the globe. They should sit together and find ways to provide education, basic health facilities, food and create opportunities of employment so that people in the backward places and nations see hope and a future which could be better in the coming years. Trying to protect their own country and the rich will one day create a situation which will be detrimental to everyone in the long run. How can the world be a better place when 1% of the most privileged own 48 percent of the wealth. This cannot be acceptable and sustainable for too long, maybe this is the biggest threat of extreme capitalism and for sure it has to change sooner than later.

It is high time that the world leaders see this earth as one big country and try to find ways to protect the natural resources, the environment, better distribution of wealth, solve problems like the one between Israel and Palestine, get constructively involved in solving regional issues rather than trying to trying to bring about regime changes which could help them get access to resources like oil or increase their sphere of influence. Only then will we see that world is a much better and safer place to stay, where the generations to come will have a much brighter future, and people with less discrimination will give less breeding ground for birth of terrorism and violence. Unless there is genuine co-operation among all the countries of the world where the leaders think and take collective decisions for the human race as a whole the world will be more and more dangerous place to live, with threats of terror strikes, natural disasters, financial meltdowns which will impact the lives of not only the poor but the rich and the developed countries also. So we all should think about what contribution we can make to keep the earth a better place to stay and a place where lives will be sustainable for the centuries to come. Leaders of the world should come together to see how they can make the world safer and better place, where kids feel safe to go the schools, the females do not have to be scared to travel at night, people will be able to get clean air to breathe and water to drink, everyone if not rich at least will be able to have two proper meals a day, instead of hatred people will try to help each other irrespective of caste, creed or religion, reduce the deaths from disease by developing better medicines and health care and if not prevent natural disaster not be the cause of bringing in disasters by destroying the very environment which makes life sustainable in this beautiful planet called earth.

I would like to conclude by giving the example of two seas, namely the Dead Sea and the Sea of Galilee. Dead Sea is a lake rather than a sea. It has very high salt content which makes no form of life possible in it. On the other hand the Sea of Galilee which is just north of Dead Sea has a lot of marine life including both plants and fishes. The interesting part is that both receive water from the river Jordan. In the case of Sea of Galilee the water from river Jordan flows into it and then flows out. The water simply passes through it keeping it vibrant and allowing life to exist and prosper. On the other hand Dead Sea is far below the sea level and so there is no outlet for the water entering it. So the stagnant water evaporates in huge amount due to the hot weather leaving behind the salt and a lot of minerals. This makes the water unfit for survival of any form of life. For humans also this thing holds true in the sense that someone may have a lot of knowledge, money, know-how, but if he tries to hold onto the same without sharing it, same will not be of much use. On the other hand if this is shared and distributed among the needy and the poor then he will get more satisfaction and happiness and will also make the life of many others more happy and vibrant.

ABOUT THE AUTHOR

The author is a professional who has worked in the private industry for the last twenty-two years and has travelled widely around the globe. He likes to observe what is happening around him and think how things could be changed for the better. He has mostly taken his inspiration from the things he has seen around from the childhood and from his interactions with people from different parts of the world.